Husbands, Lovers, And Other Sorrows

Very Short Stories for People With

Very Little Time

True Stories Retold by

Bette Epstein

BETTE EPSTEIN

Other Books by Bette Epstein:

A Time to Mourn, Poems, 2000.
And When I Am Old, Poems, compiled 1992-2011
The Jews Harp, A Tale of Five Women 2010

Copyright © 2011 Bette Epstein
ISBN-13: 978-1467950015
Printed by Create Space
Charleston, SC 29418 USA

HUSBANDS, LOVERS, AND OTHER SORROWS

BETTE EPSTEIN

INTRODUCTION

I have started this book a dozen times over the past six years and each time, I've put it on hold for "another time." Only today did I realize why I had never completed it. Not because I felt it was unimportant, not really that at all, but because it was too painful for me to write about the great love of my life. And — how can a writer have any integrity in her work on a subject she is so familiar with if she cannot open her own heart and be part of the story. Just this afternoon while sitting outside my favorite coffee shop, my mind wandered to these stories and I knew it was time.

I have been a romance junkie since I was a child, hiding in the closet late at night with a flashlight, reading my older sister's Love Comics. I knew some day my prince would come. I knew he would be totally in love with me; we would make a beautiful life together, have clever children and we would laugh and make love and see the world together. Well, it wasn't quite like that...but one day he did appear. He was almost exactly as I had imagined him to be.

Then there were great years, and good years, and clever children, and sad years, and then it was over. I couldn't possibly remember that part of my life as anything except a blessing and with great joy, and now it is almost as if it had been a dream. I never told anyone how much I love him, loved him. He was the only one who knew. I was afraid if others knew...and he was taken from me... that they would feel sorry for me. I have a tremendous fear of pity, of sympathy. Afraid that if I ever allow others to know my real heart... and someone should dare hug me and say, "There, there, I understand..." that I will be lost forever in an abyss of sympathy. But today I take that chance and somewhere in this book I will write about him.

Because sharing is so difficult for me I respect women and men who love and admit a love that takes them to another level of their humanness. I have been there; I just couldn't talk about it. And, oh, how I've always admired those who could. I am a woman who loves men, all sorts of men, for a variety of reasons. I am totally accepting of their "manliness" and there have been many wonderful men in my life in the past few years, each one more precious than the last — and even as healed as I think I am — I pray there will never be another man whom I love so much that I want to keep those feelings a secret even from myself.

The following stories are all true. They are from clients, friends, women on planes, trains, subways, buses, conferences and strangers in coffee shops. Important details have been changed to protect the identity of the women who shared their loves with me, but everything from the heart has been left as it was at the moment it was told. The stories are written here in a "stream of consciousness" style, flowing freely from my memory of the telling. I am especially grateful to the women; those now over the age of seventy-five, who blessed me with their loves because we tend to forget, categorize, and dismiss the depth of love and romance in older people as we do the intensity of teenage love.

This book was never intended as therapy but to reaffirm for women of every path that they are not alone in their need to love and be loved. I think of it as a gathering of women somewhere safe where we take turns sharing our stories of love lost and found and sometimes lost again — and when the telling is done, we hug and hold one-another and say, "I know — I understand." In spite of my own fears, I know it's okay to be powerful in love, to be empowered by it and to be vulnerable in it. I'm sorry I cannot tell, in this little book, the remaining hundreds of stories stored in my memory files.
Perhaps another time...

BETTE EPSTEIN

DEDICATION

To each of the women who shared their stories with me... I honor you by dedicating this book to you. Thank you for trusting me to retell your stories as you told them to me and I hope I have done you proud.

To each of the women who shared their stories with me... I honor you by dedicating this book to you. Thank you for trusting me to retell your stories as you told them to me and I hope I have done you proud.

BETTE EPSTEIN

CONTENTS

The

Stories

BETTE EPSTEIN

DARLENE

October 3, 1998
Norman, Oklahoma
Friend's House Party
Country girl, stocky, blond, sweet face

We were both sixteen when we got married. I was pregnant not because we had a lot of hot sex but because we didn't know how not to get pregnant. West Texas is full of little towns were the main occupation is secrets and religion. I was born in 1960 and because of our church; we were still not allowed to watch television in 1976. Not that I would have learned much about birth control back then on TV.

Steve and I were typical of the kids I grew up with — horny and stupid. He really believed that if he just put the head in and quickly pulled it out when he came, that I could not get pregnant. We didn't dare ask anyone, not even our best friends because everyone loved to gossip. The first year we were married, we had Katy and the next year, Patty.

1

By the age of twenty, we were broke, still in love, and the parents of two beautiful little girls. We moved to Oklahoma to another small town and things got better. I got a job in a day care and Steve got a really good job. We saved up enough money to buy a house and we just got happier and happier.

Things rocked along great for a lot of years. We became active in the community; going to rodeos and church socials. We never fought, didn't drink or smoke anything, and just loved being together and taking care of our now almost grown daughters. I had always been somewhat of a tomboy and hated being confined to an indoor job all day. So when I heard of this job with the highway department, striping roads, I went right over and applied.

At thirty-six I was strong and able to do just about anything a young man could do, even lift and tote. They hired me and I loved the job. I had been working there six months when I met Eric. He was twenty-one and loaded with testosterone. This is not the end of the story, not even close. We started this hot and heavy thing that totally got out of control. This was all new for me for Steve had always been a very tender, caring lover but without a lot of passion. Well, you know when you're over thirty and into some hot, lustful, exciting, and illicit relationship, you just can't get enough. I took lots of stupid chances to be with him and soon began to think I was in love. I was pregnant. Then I got scared. Then he got scared. Meanwhile, I was getting bigger and beginning to show. We decided I should get a divorce and we would get married.

So I told Steve everything. I was crying and bawling and had snot running all down my face, mascara smeared everywhere. He looked at me for a while, didn't say nothing. Walked outside and pretty soon I heard a gunshot. I ran outside, terrified. There was Steve, shooting tin cans off the fence just like he did every time he got nervous about something. He turned around and came inside. "You think about it, Darlene."

I told him I would bring Eric to meet him and he agreed. Eric was scared shitless, but he came. Steve didn't act ugly at all, just sort of detached as if he was talking to one of our girls boyfriends. I had told both of them that I was going to have this baby natural and I needed a birthing partner. I guess I shouldn't have been surprised that Eric didn't feel he was ready to do that, so Steve agreed he would. I was to continue to live with Steve until Eric could find us a place and the divorce was final. I know this all sounds surreal but as God is my witness, this is what happened.

Weeks later I went to work and Eric didn't show up. I called his house and the phone rang and rang and no answer. I went over there after work that day and there was no sign that anyone had ever lived there. Lock, stock, and barrel.

Gone like the wind. I didn't tell Steve that Eric had run out on me. I just said it is over. Then I told him I would leave because I didn't want to give up my baby and I didn't expect him to raise it with me.

He just held me. "Darlene, everybody makes mistakes. We've grown up together. We were both raised to believe that forgiveness is the next thing to being like the Lord and I don't want to sound like no Bible-thumper, but I still believe that. I can love that baby. It won't know no difference in whether I'm its daddy or Eric is. If you don't tell nobody, I won't tell. You pray on it tonight."

Before I made up my mind, I tried everything to find Eric to make sure he wasn't coming back. He hadn't left a trace.

The baby came in October and she was as beautiful as the other two girls and we became grandparent that same fall. When I was a little kid, my Mama would say, "Darlene, when life hands you lemons, make lemonade," and I thought I just might have to do that but you know what, with the love of Steve, I got a lot more than lemonade.

It's been three years and Steve has kept his promise and we have fallen in love all over again and it's better than when we were sixteen because now we know how blessed we are. We sleep all wrapped up in each other like we're afraid some thief will come in the night and take one of us but it's not about fear. It's about knowing our union was tested and we came to the ragged edge of losing a lifetime of love.

BONNIE

October 27, 1999
Indianapolis International Airport
Food Court
Short, athletic, very blond
Lives in Detroit

I was nineteen and mad at the world. My mother had run off with some bad-ass trucker, leaving me to finish school as a boarder in my aunt's house.

I knew who Delbert was because I had gone to high school with his sister; but I hadn't paid any attention to him ever and didn't intend to. He just sort of sneaked up on me, flattered me, and promised to change my life.

We would move to the city, he said, maybe even find my mother. I went with him, married him. We moved to Detroit and he took a job in one of the car factories and I worked the line at General Electric. He wasn't exactly mean to me that first year but I knew he was sleeping with the woman who lived in the apartment upstairs from us.

5

He worked nights, I worked days and so he had all the time in the world to be doing her. I don't even remember being mad. He wasn't much of a lover, just always hard. I can't recall a day during our marriage when he didn't want sex.

Well, a year after we moved up there, I was pregnant. Thank God. I hated that line. I loved being a mother and was determined to do a better job of it than my own mother had done with me. I don't know if I ever learned to love Delbert of not. I just got used to him. He drank too much and when he did, he got real stupid and mean. I had to go to the neighborhood bar most every Friday night and bring his silly ass home. I tried to raise my kids with some pride but their father made them ashamed most of the time.

The older he got, he meaner he got. He had always hated black people, used the "N" word all the time. He didn't say much about it around me and the kids until all the Civil Rights stuff was on TV and then he became so vocal, the boys had to ask him to stop.

When our last child was in high school, I went back to work. This time I took an office job and my boss was a very sweet, handsome black man. Delbert about shit. He complained for days that he didn't want his wife taking no orders from a black man. Well, he didn't say "black."

Soon that wasn't all I was taking from Clif. We fell in love and I was in heaven. He was also married and had grown kids and, as I did, and didn't want to hurt anyone by divorcing. So we went on like that for twenty years. I had a girlfriend to cover for me and we managed to see each other a couple of times a week and go away for a weekend once in a while. I really believe he was my destiny. He was definitely the love of my life.

One day I came home from work early and caught Delbert in bed with the wife of our eldest son. She cried and said he had forced her and I believe her. I was so mad at him that I could have killed him. But fate took care of that for me.

A week later he was working on his car; had crawled up under it without anyone to watch the jack for him. Well, the jack gave out and the car fell, crushing him to death. We had never gone to church and the children thought it was sweet of me to find a minister to preach at Delbert's funeral. No one ever knew about Clif, nor that the black minister who preached at Delbert's funeral, was Clif's brother.

I've never shed a tear over Delbert, but sometimes I smile myself to sleep thinking about how Delbert must have been spinning around in his grave when he looked up and saw that black face. Two years after Delbert died, Clif had a stroke and was never able to speak again. I managed to become friends with his wife so that I could help take care of him until he died three years ago. He visits me in my dreams most every night. I will always love him.

BETTE EPSTEIN

JACKIE

September 23, 2003
Dallas, Texas
Brookhaven College Piano class
Average, puffy, funny
Grew up in Waco

*I*t was back in the 80s when everyone I knew was wild and crazy. I was twenty-seven, single, and living not too far from downtown where I worked and right in the middle of all the singles bars, or as they were called then, the meat markets. Women were actually called "head" in those days and the bars were packed from Thursday until Sunday brunch with young people on the make. No one thought less of you for sleeping with a guy you didn't know; it was simply the times. AIDS was still mostly among the gays and just about any STDs could still be knocked out with a big dose of penicillin.

Thursday was just a warm-up for the real crowds which came out on Friday. Big hair, big earrings, big skirts,

9

huge belts, wide shoulders, and no panties were the way to go. It was April, raining like pouring piss out of a boot, and instead of taking a taxi like I usually did when I knew I would get drunk, I decided to stay sober and drive my car. I started cruising and decided I wasn't ready for noise and so I stopped for my first beer at Joe Miller's. A dump, really, but one held in great reverence by Ad people who worked in the area....writers, radio and TV personalities, and tall blondes. The restrooms were covered with a continuing story instead of graffiti and I added a couple of lines when I went in to pee. I cut a pretty fine figure that night and all the heads turned as I walked in but I couldn't make out any faces because of the semi-darkness. I found an empty seat at the bar and made it mine. I started with a beer, figuring I would only be there for a few minutes. Well, conversations heated up and I ended up in a booth with five guys I had never seen before. One of them, a guy named Tom, really piqued my interest because he had the fullest head of black curls I had ever seen And...He was fairly interesting, obviously finding me attractive.

A couple of hours later we laughed together and by then I was too drunk to drive so I gave him my keys. He drove us to my apartment and since he was almost as drunk as I was, I invited him to spend the night. We fell asleep in my bed after a drunken attempt to have sex. I had forgotten to close the shades and so, at sunlight, I was awakened. I sat up in bed and saw two startling things: the man next to me he had short blond hair...and...My cat was wrestling with something that looked like a dead rat. The blond man was also wearing a wedding ring, and on the bedside table were a few miscellaneous teeth attached to wire things. I jumped out of bed and surveyed the situation.

The fast moves I had made did not disturb Tom at all as he was snoring with his mouth wide open, making a sound somewhat like I would imagine a $10 chainsaw trying to take out a 200 year old hard rock maple tree. Little Pussy was having a great time with this rat, which upon careful examination, turned out to be the full curly black wig of my guest. For one brief moment I was paralyzed with indecision then I quickly gathered up my clothes, left the room, closing Little Pussy, the dead rat, and my guest up in the bedroom.

I went to the kitchen, took my notepad, and wrote a note which I slipped under the door. "Sorry, Emergency. Had to go to work. Lock up on your way out. Yellow cab responds very quickly in this neighborhood; their number by phone. My mom is stopping by about ten." On my way to my car I stopped downstairs and used the pay phone to call my own apartment in order to wake him up. Joe Miller's closed that next year and I will always wonder how the story on the bathroom walls ended.

And me, oh, yeah, I grew up, stopped drinking, moved to Tyler when I got married and became a soccer mom...blond ponytail and all. Recently I saw that movie, *The Banger Sisters*... and for one whole afternoon I really longed for my old wild life.

ELIZABETH

November 6, 2008
Austin, Texas
Whole Foods Waiting for Massage
Tiny, elegant, literate, pretty
Grew up in San Antonio, Texas

*N*ow that I'm over my crush on him I can tell you about it. It was over just last year. I'm 88 now and he was 47. He had moved into the rent house next door to me during one of the worse thunderstorms I can remember. Don't know why the stubborn fool didn't call off the move, but there he was out in all that mess with his helpers, moving a bunch of junkie old furniture into that beautiful house. He would smile and wave when we happened to see one-another but I didn't see him to talk to until one day when it was again pouring rain.

I was walking out to the car to go to church. He came over to the edge of the driveway and asked if I wanted him to drive me. I was incensed. I let him know in no uncertain terms that I got along just fine before he moved into that house, and, by God, I could still drive myself in the rain. He must have thought me a total old angry fool, but he didn't show it. As much as I wanted to sit next to him in that little sports car, I wasn't about to give in to any aging stereotyping. If I give in to one little thing pretty soon I will act old, feel old and then it will all be over.

I had a terrible, marvelous crush on him. I found out his name was Wil (with one L) Hansen. I ate, drank, and slept my fantasy about him. I had a delicious scene that played over and over in my head. He would come over to my house to bring in firewood (yes, I would allow him to do that), and after he gets the fire started, we share a bottle of wine and I serve those stuffed mushrooms I do so well. Then we have this wonderful, intimate, and soft spoken conversation about life and literature and art and he would touch my shoulder as he gets up to stoke the fire. I would tell him about my trips to Egypt and India and the men who loved me when I was seeing the world alone. He would be mesmerized by the stories and my seductive voice. He will take my hand in his and look into my face and we will know we are in love...like star-crossed lovers.

He lived there one year and after about three months we actually did form a bond very much like my fantasy; we established a beautiful ritual of friendship. Once, when he was in my house, we laughed about something and he took my face into his hands and told me I am ageless. He said he would like to see pictures of me when I was in my youth. I told him I am in my youth and we both laughed again. Then we hugged for a long time. Many nights he would come over with wine and a book he was reading and we would stay up late talking books and writers. I wanted him to tell me who the small woman in the blue car was, the one with the baby who slept through all the crying she did when she left his house, but he never did. I wanted to hear who the coarse, chain-smoking, tall, skinny cursing woman who laughs with him late into the night is. But he never revealed her name.

The small woman continued to visit and the baby grew into a toddler, walking to the car sometimes. The cursing woman was replaced by a rather robust Mexican woman who cooked for him when she wasn't singing. Many times I would hear her singing. Well, she was more pleasant than the cursing one. He never shared with me anything about his real life, just the books and trips and dreams. He was a very secretive Scorpio, you know.

I'm glad he didn't tell me he was leaving for I would have been sad longer. I didn't realize he had moved out while I was at church until I saw the note taped to my front door. "Dear Elisabeth. Time to move on, the air is getting thin here. You were the best part of my stay in Austin. Left some books for you in the kitchen. Have a nice life." Didn't even sign his name! Never saw him again...but I think one day he will come back. We will sit on the porch and I will recite Kavafy's Ithaca all the way through for him and he will squeeze my hand and smile.

CHASTITY

April 22, 2001
Rockwall, Texas
Starbucks Coffee
Sitting outside being friendly
Rode hard, formerly awesome
Grew up in Kansas

O h, God, I love this man. The first time I saw him was at a picnic in Manhattan, Kansas. He was tall, dark, and the most handsome man I had ever seen. I was tall, skinny, thin brown hair, and freckles... plus, I was a single mom trying to raise a child all by myself. I didn't dare look at him. Why would a guy like that pay attention to a cashier from the feed and seed store? He walked past us, my mom, my baby Lolly, and me, and I didn't dare look up. Then he turned around and came back to our blanket, reached out for my hand, and asked if I would like to go for a walk with him.

Mom said she would look after Lolly and as I looked back at her, she gave me a wink of approval. It was the 50s and life was pretty tame in the Midwest. He asked me for a date every night for the next week. We went to see movies with Marilyn Monroe, Tab Hunter, James Dean, Sal Mineo, Natalie Wood, Rock Hudson, and Debbie Reynolds. We went to all of those movies so I wouldn't have to talk to him. If we talked at all it was about the movies and what it must be like to be such a glamorous person.

I was afraid that if I talked he would think I was not only unattractive, but dumb. I hadn't been anywhere, or done anything. After a month we hugged and kissed a lot but neither of us ever initiated sex and so our whole dating was pure and sweet and hesitant. It didn't take long before we decided we wanted to be together for the rest of our lives and so we had a storybook wedding with Lolly as my flower girl and she held the rings. She enjoyed Max more than her own dad because he paid attention to her, made her feel special.

Our wedding night was uneventful because we were so clumsy, but once we got the hang of it everything was just great. My first marriage had been because of Lolly, to a boy who thought making love was getting a hard-on and poking me, so I didn't really understand that it was something to be enjoyed until I was with Max. We learned to make love like we were gliding around the dance floor to Bob Wills. Seldom has there been a day since we married that we haven't made love before drifting off to sleep in each other's arms.

Ten years later we moved to Dallas and being loved by Max had made me a lot better looking. We made quite a splash with the artist crowd in the late 60s. We made a very exciting life for ourselves in Dallas. Max was the darling of all the galleries with his paintings and in the 70s I bought my own gallery, showing only Western art. Being from Kansas seemed to give me certain credibility. Then Max started acting and got a lot of good parts. Sometimes we would look at ourselves in the mirror and say, "who are those people?"

We were invited to everything in this city and on Sunday mornings we rushed to see how many pictures of us would be in the *People* section. We really got addicted to being beautiful and adored, just as we got addicted to drinking, doing drugs, shopping, being seen at all the right places. Lolly had grown up and moved to her own place, leaving us to be totally self-indulgent. There was never a weekend without parties; local politicians, strippers, Dallas Cowboys, celebrities, everybody getting high together. I guess we were seduced by our vanity. Throughout all of this foolishness, we never fell out of love, and never cheated on each other. Stoned or drunk, we still fell asleep cuddled up together.

Then it happened. I woke up one day with my hands so stiff I couldn't make a fist. My knees were swollen beyond recognition. Then I turned to Max and said, "Baby, look what's happened to me." He held my hands in his and said, "Why?" I told him I thought it was our lifestyle, this destructive roller-coaster of fun we were having for so many years. So I went to the doctor for all the tests and everything wrong with my body could be directly related to the way we lived. I had just run out of resistance.

Lolly had gone back to Kansas to go to Art School and so we followed her there. Max and I went back to the park where we had taken that first walk together. I know our lifestyle could have made an invalid of me before I was 50.

And I don't think I could have changed if we had stayed in Dallas...It was just too seductive. So, I'm glad I got a little sick before I got real sick. We are happy here. Not like wild and crazy happy, but calm and smart happy. And...We are still in love.

NICOLE

May 21, 2002
Ft. Worth, Texas
Book Club Group
Anglo who looks Latin with blue eyes
Grew up in Arlington, Texas

I'm fifty-nine now. I'm pretty normal considering how I used to be. I grew up in Catholic schools through the twelfth grade. I wouldn't suggest anyone do that to their kids. Of course, things were different in the late fifties. The nuns still wore habits and slammed your hands with a ruler and no one cared. They gave me a lot of twisted ideas about sex. I can't fault them. That was their job. I just wish my parents had been able to think for themselves. I went to college and got a degree in Home Economics. I always knew I would get married right out of college and so I was prepared for it.

I met and married Tracy the first year after graduation. He was exactly the man I had in mind when I used to sit in the back of the classroom, daydreaming about the husband I would one day find. I think I was really in love with Tracy. I believe I am now and I know he must have loved me to put up with me for all of those years and not leave. I had a real aversion to sex or any sex talk or any affection that might lead to sex. And I hated being married; it wasn't at all what I wanted it to be. I did the best I could. I learned to give parties, I was good to my in-laws, I did all of the correct and proper things a good wife does, except enjoy sex. I absolutely hated kissing.

But the twisted part of this story is that I had relationships with other men....lots of them. And somehow I managed to have sex with Tracy enough to give birth twice. I liked being a mom; even did all the expected things like Scouting and the PTA. I wasn't a total wash, but terribly confused. I had the idea that marriage and sex were going to be romantic and they just weren't! How could they be when there were so many things to do, so much to take care of? I had led a very sheltered life. I was not prepared for reality. I didn't like it. I wanted romance and flowers and gifts and words of adoration. I wanted boyfriends. But I still didn't want sex.

So...things just seemed to take on a life of their own. I would meet a man at a party or in a group (I preferred a married man because I knew single ones would call your house and cause trouble) and somehow let him know I was interested in him. We would begin to meet in another part of the city for lunch. We would have intimate conversations, love letters, romantic gifts, touching fingertips during meals, statements of love.

Then, when these men would reach a boiling point, I would end it. I was never anything but beautiful, so the seduction was easy enough that I didn't have to wait very long before I had another romance going. Sometimes I had more than one at a time.

The thrill of getting caught might have been a part of it too. Sometimes after going to confession I would be determined to give up my romantic life but then I would get up one day feeling ugly and unloved and almost like magic, someone new would appear, ready to love me. I continued this behavior for over fifteen years. Tracy had long given up on having any sort of normal sex life with me. I gave in to him on his birthday, Christmas and Easter, and sometimes on Thanksgiving. But...I still didn't kiss him.

On January 1, 1999, Tracy got up early and started to pack. The kids were long gone from our immediate lives and there was no real reason for him to continue to stay with me. He was leaving. Getting a divorce, he said. Said he had always loved me but needed a real wife, one who would be tender with him and hold him and, yes, even kiss him sometimes.

I didn't try to stop him. Then I got drunk and stayed drunk for a month. And I found a therapist and for six months she dug around in my poor confused psyche, trying to help me. I wanted my man back and I tried every traditional or alternative therapy I had heard of and after all of the work and tears all we could ever come up with was illusion. I had an illusion of how marriage would be and could not, did not, make that quantum leap from what I thought it was to what it really was and I was not willing to settle for less than a Hollywood marriage...well, Hollywood of a long time ago.

On Tracy's birthday eight months later I went looking for him. When I found him, I asked him to kiss me and he did. I think for the first time in my life, I actually felt passion...a real passion, not something I made up. We make love everyday now and it is constant struggle with me to stay in the present and not beat myself up for my past. I think I've forgiven myself...it feels like I have.

JOHANNA

May 13, 2002
Workshop to learn about
Radical Attachment Disorder
Dallas, Texas
Grew up in Irving, Texas
Athletic blonde

When he said he was from Bosnia, I should have run like a scared rabbit. But what did I know, or even care. All I knew was that he was at my favorite jazz bar which probably meant he loved jazz too and...That he was outrageously good looking. I was also impressed that he spoke English with just a trace of an accent. When the band took a break and the D.J. came on, he asked me to dance. I found out that his name was Sasha (his ancestry was actually Russian and this is a nickname for Alexandria, his great-grandfather). We danced fast, slow, wild, easy, Latin. Never left the dance floor; even danced to jazz. His eyes were as blue as the New Mexico sky, surrounded by black curls of eyelash.

25

He asked me to marry him there that night on the dance floor. I said yes. We stayed together all night and the next morning found a Justice of the Peace to perform the marriage ceremony. We lied and said we had known each other for a year because we were afraid he would lecture us about what we were doing. I should have stayed for the lecture. The first six months were beyond bliss. Then what had been more heat than light became more light than heat...the honeymoon was over and reality had come to stay. In this new light I was faced with what the horrors of war had done to my man.

He was there for everything...all the slaughter. He hid in a barn when the whole village he lived in was gunned down. We can't go horseback riding (one of my favorite things) because the smell of straw or hay will send him into convulsions. At night he sits and rocks back and forth and makes sounds so eerie that I have to cover my head. He can't work. Loses one job after another because of his temper which will go off over some little thing, then he will curse and run away. When these episodes are over he will come home to me to be held and rocked until he falls asleep, exhausted. I often go to work leaving him in the bed curled into a tight little fetal position and eight hours later come back and he is still there.

We have gone for therapy. I still go to therapy. He feels if he is a real man he must defeat his demons by himself. I thought things were getting better when he got on his meds. He would leave the house in the mornings in good spirit but by late afternoon he might return in the form of some monster I can't identify...A new one each day.

I'm turning thirty this year and I want to have children in the next ten years but he is afraid he has some gene that makes him crazy and he will pass it on, so we don't have sex because he doesn't trust birth control. Making love with him used to be great. He was a tender, passionate, eager lover and we were perfectly matched but that is over now.

One doctor diagnosed him as having Radical Attachment Disorder and without thinking, I went along with that and for months we went through all those exercises to learn to bond. Until one day I put my brain into the ON position and realized he bonds just fine, it's these monsters with machine guns that he can't get out of his head and the bodies of little children and women with their guts slashed open.

How do we remove those memories! How can I help him? How can I help myself so that I don't give up on him? He is the other half of me and I am dying trying to keep him alive.

BETTE EPSTEIN

LESLEE

April 22, 2010
Mid-flight to Los Angeles
Chatting with seatmate
Short, dark hair and eyes, cute
Grew up in Ohio

I wasn't a child when we met I was almost thirty and had had plenty of relationship experience. But he totally intrigued me. We lived next door in the apartments and once I had met him I found myself making up any crazy excuse I could to go to his apartment. He was an artist and worked at home and although he was always welcoming, I knew I should call first. But I never did. I just couldn't get enough of him. After six months of dogging him, I convinced him that we were in love. He hesitated for he had been married twice already and felt he was not suited for commitment. I finally wore him down and after he said he loved me, our lovemaking escalated to the most passionate sexual experience of my life, even to this day. I

29

didn't want to be with anyone else and didn't want him to either.

I gave up all of my girlfriends, my parents, my hobbies. He kept trying to maintain some personal space but I wouldn't have it. I wanted him to focus all of his time and attention on me. After a year I convinced him to move in with me and we bought a house together. I was immediately pregnant and so we had a quickie wedding, planning to do a big splashy thing later. I immediately began nesting. He continued to try to find personal time, work time, and workout time. I couldn't stand it. I bought a phone for his car and would call him and talk the entire time he was away from me. I was, frankly, making him nuts. Our sex life came to a standstill even though I wanted it more when I was pregnant than before but he kept trying to get away from me.

After the baby came...a beautiful girl...my nesting instincts became stronger and my attention to Trevor lessened...much to his delight. But, I also stopped being any sort of companion to him. He hadn't wanted this baby and try as he might, he just couldn't figure out what his role here was. So we fought. I wanted him to only want to be a father and husband; to constantly shop with me for furniture and paint. He was trying to sell his paintings and establish himself in different markets with his work.

Sometimes I would hear him crying himself to sleep. I knew he was in deep depression about this life we had created but I refused to acknowledge how desperately he wanted a different life. I didn't want to talk about it.

Sometimes in an attempt to be a better husband he would ask me to get a sitter and go with him to concerts, or to bike around the lake, or take dance lessons.

He once asked me to leave the baby with my mom and go away with him to a motel for a weekend. How ridiculous; I'm a MOM. Moms don't go away for a weekend of lovemaking. I started telling him he didn't love the baby. He did love her, he just didn't know what I wanted of him as a father and I couldn't communicate that. In fact, I didn't think I should have to explain it to him, it should come naturally.

So we started to fight most every day. I hated him. He hated me. I loved him, he loved me. We were a mess. One Saturday I told him that if he went bike riding around the lake instead of mowing the lawn, he should just not ever come home again. And he didn't. It was over.

If I had not had the baby I would have killed myself but I had to stay alive for her. Trevor became a better father. When he would come for her, we never made eye contact. There with such a painful scar in the energy surrounding us that we could not look at one another. I hope someday I will stop loving him, will stop believing I brought this failure up on myself; that I forced my baby's father to leave her.

Sometimes I dream about him coming home to me. That when we are in our fifties I will be sitting out on the porch swing one sunny afternoon and I will look up and see Trevor walking up the walk with a bouquet of Black-eyed Susan's in his hand (that is what he always called me when we were in love) and he will say, "Any pretty girls live here who want to try it again." Until he marries someone else, I guess I can keep that dream.

NORA ANNE

December 9, 1997
Dallas, Texas
Next to her getting a manicure
Chocolate cookie color
Grew up in Oak cliff, Texas

$\mathcal{I}$ married him when I was eighteen and he was 32. I was one of his students in high school and as soon as I graduated, he told me he loved me. We dated for a month and Momma gave me a big wedding. I don't know why any mother would do such a thing. Or, at least, I didn't know then but as I got older, I began to realize a lot about my mom and why she did the things she did. I was one of five kids. My dad was a drunk who appeared in our lives about five times a year.

Mom worked as a maid in the home of the owners of one of the most elite clothing stores in Dallas. They really worked her, too. She was totally devoted to them and the worst days of my life were the holidays when she would dress us up like little black puppets, take us to the Christmas parties they gave, and everyone would fuss over those little "nigra" children. This was in the late Fifties.

Mom was such a strong, resourceful woman. I don't think we went without much. She was a dedicated Christian and everything she did, she gave Jesus credit for. If I had been born with blonde hair and blue eyes, she would have said Jesus wanted it that way. She played the organ at church and sometimes I still pretend that I can see her up there in front of the church, playing. I can see her arms in that pink organza dress and hear her singing *IN THE SWEET BY AND BY* as the pastor gave the altar call. I can even see the tears running down her face as she sings about her Sweet Jesus. Sometimes she would bend over and wipe her tears on her shoulder but she never missed a note.

She never asked anything of me but to be good and do my best. When the kids were about to get bused to North Dallas, she managed to come up with the money for all three of my kids to go to Catholic schools. And we sure weren't Catholic.

Daddy was a charming scoundrel and she never stopped loving him. My heart still fills when I remember those times when he did come home. He would walk into that little house and suddenly it would he become a palace. Our king was home. Momma never yelled me for loving him so much for she loved him too. I would see the softening of her posture, the mellowness that came into her eyes when he appeared. She had a special night gown and perfume safely hidden in the back of the closet for when he came home. Little girls have a way of knowing a lot about their Mommas.

So now that I'm old enough to have a better understanding I can know why she encouraged me to marry Nathan. He was an educator, something she had always admired. And, he didn't drink. She saw him as someone who could improve my life, give me stability. Until I was forty, I didn't really know what being in love meant, so I don't know if I had ever been IN love with Nathan, but I did love him. He became a politician during the first five years of our marriage and started going to Washington a lot, so I saw very little of him. I gave birth three times and he didn't appear one time of the hospital for either of those births, at least not until I was out of recovery. When he did appear it was always with gifts and cards and remorse.

What Momma didn't know about men was that there were a lot of addictions worse than alcohol. Well, at least as bad. Nathan was a sex addict. Even if we made love in the morning, he was out by noon looking for someone else. He once confided that he thought by marrying someone fourteen years his junior, he would be able to maintain his attention to me and no one else, but he quickly realized this addiction had nothing to do with me...it was his need to be validated as desirable by strangers.

I stayed in denial for fifteen years and then with therapy, I was able to ask him to leave. He spent a lot of time and treatment centers but he had no real desire to change. He never remarried and that is a good thing. We stayed in touch until the kids finished college and I expect to see him at weddings and births, but I don't look forward to it. I still love him. Yes, I have a husband...a wonderful, stable, very loving man, but the little girl in me still loves Nathan. I don't long for him, but I know if he were ever in trouble, I would go to him...even in the middle of the night... even if he called when I was lying next to my man.

ROBIN

September 9, 2006
Dallas, Texas
After Yoga class for Tea
Painfully thin looking, but muscular. Blond and beautiful
Grew up in Dallas, Texas

Compared to the way my kids are growing up in the world of cyberspace, I guess being born in 1962 would be considered pretty dull. My brother and I had each other and the kids on our block for entertainment. We grew up on a dead end street where most everyone was Catholic and there were over one hundred kids on our block. My bro Pete and I couldn't wait to get out the house on holidays and weekends to meet the other kids in the "clubhouse". It was in this maze of refrigerator boxes and discarded wood that I learned all about life, sex, politics and the lies our parents told. We showed each other our private parts, held the little kids when they got hurt and kept each other's secrets.

Since I was two years old, I loved Sammy. He was a couple of years older and he was nice to me. Sammy was one of thirteen kids who lived five houses down in a huge old two-story brownstone. His parents were very active in their church and they did not let the Catholics or Jews into their house. They belonged to a religion his grandpa had started and they believed everything the Bible said just as it said it. They didn't go to doctors; the girls couldn't cut their hair nor wear make-up or jewelry and no dating without a chaperone. I don't know how they ended up in our neighborhood for it was mostly real liberal people; one of our neighbors even had meetings of the Peoples Party once a month in their house. Oh, yes, I forgot to mention, they didn't use birth control either...in case you hadn't figured that out.

As we grew older, Sammy and I grew closer. My folks wouldn't have minded for they figured this puppy love would end soon enough, but this wasn't puppy love, this was real. We could read each other's minds and finish each other's sentences even before we were ten years old. We were in love and all the kids on the block knew it. After Sammy was in puberty, he was not allowed to play with the other kids anymore. He had "chores" to do every day after school and on weekends.

So we learned to be real sneaky and being sneaky meant being alone together and being alone together meant heavy petting. By the time I was sixteen he was about to graduate from high school and had been accepted into a private religious college in Tennessee. You can guess the rest of the story. Before the end of that summer, I was pregnant.

I told my folks and they made a plan. As I was starting to "show", Mom and I would go away for a while and she would come back with the new baby. She was young, she wanted to protect me, and she didn't want to give up her first grandchild. Besides, she loved Sammy, too. And that's what we did.

When Sammy came back that first summer, he took one look at my "little sister" Emily, (who looked just like him) and he had sort of a mental breakdown. He had to be hospitalized for a long time and, not being able to handle the shame of his illness, his family moved away from our neighborhood.

I finished high school, went to Vanderbilt but couldn't stand being away from my Emily and so I went home to my parents. I never dated. Sammy really was my one true love. I wrote to him every day that we were not together, volumes of journals about Emily and how much I missed him.

When Emily was four we were walking up to the ice cream parlor near our house and all of a sudden I was aware of a car slowly getting closer and closer to us so I grabbed her up and started running. Sammy stopped the car, got out and called to me. I had no point of reference for this. Since his breakdown I had not had a fantasy about him coming back. I fainted, dropping Emily to the ground.

When I opened my eyes, he was there, holding me and talking softly to Emily so that she would not be afraid. He held the two of us as we sat on that grassy strip near the ice cream store and we talked and talked so long, Mom came looking for us. She had told Sammy where to find us and was delighted to see our joy.

We worked things out. My folks were wonderful. Sammy and I had three more children; we still finish one-another's sentences...and...Just like in the movies, we lived happily ever-after.

MELINDA

October 30, 1995
Dallas, Texas
Bagel store on Lovers Lane
Cute, blond, dancer type, very Anglo
Grew up in Dallas

The first time I saw him he was already married. He'd been married less than a year and already having an affair with my roommate, Zoe. Zoe was this ethereal, whispery-voiced dance teacher who shared an apartment with me in the summer of '83. She had known Jared through some theater group but had been living away from Fort Worth for a couple of years, during which time he fell in love and got married. Well, I assume he fell in love. He did get married. He was tall, handsome, strong, articulate, and with skin the color of a slightly burned chocolate cookie.

41

Mostly I remember his hands...huge but smooth as silk. Zoe said when she and Jared saw each other after all that time, they realized they had more in common than they had ever known and so, had to consummate this...whatever. It didn't seem to bother either of them that he was recently married. He actually lived at his writing studio half the time, being creative, you know. Sometimes he would come to the apartment to get Zoe and I would just stand there, mesmerized and drooling. She is an artist, as well as a dancer, and often would show me drawings she had done of him "in repose." Once, I think her drawings almost made my heart stop.

He worked three days at a week as an English professor at a local college (which shall remain unnamed) and spent the other two days entertaining Zoe. I don't think I was jealous. Probably never even thought I had a chance with him since I was so pasty white and blonde and certainly not a babe. Zoe and Jared even worked out together. So, years passed. That summer she moved to Florida and he divorced and moved to New York. I moved to Dallas.

It was October '91; one of those balmy days when you think maybe there really is a God. I was sitting in Massimo Cafe with friends after a late movie. We were laughing and being stupid when I looked up toward the front door of the restaurant and there he was. Our eyes met. He recognized me. I wiped the drool off my chin, got up, and went to greet him. We hugged and he gently kissed my cheek and introduced me to the woman he was with. We exchanged a few pleasantries and I went back to my friends and their teasing. I had to go to my car to get something; he followed me out (without his friend), and asked me if he could see me later that night. I gave him my address and we made a time.

At midnight thirty he arrived at my door. He came in, closed the front door, moved me gently to the stairs, and lifted me to the second step where I would be tall enough to kiss him. He moved to me slowly up the stairs, two steps and many passionate kisses until we reach the top. When we were inside the bedroom I started to undress and he said, "No, wait, I'll do that." It would not suffice to say this experience was bliss. It was more like a waltz, every few steps punctuated by passionate kisses.

We continued to explore, make love, glide, slide, and be in love until way past first light, drifting off into a magical sleep, awakening, and continuing all day and deep into the next night. Two days later he went back to New York.

Except for a few love poems and notes exchanged, I have never needed to be with him again. I don't feel we have any unfinished business and, frankly, I want this memory to remain untarnished by life. I think we feel the same about what happened. It was something that had to be; a desire built up over years of fantasy and longing, but way too strong and hard and deep to make a lifetime of. I suppose history could repeat itself, but if it doesn't, that's okay too.

BETTE EPSTEIN

TAMMY

May 17, 2005
Kerrville Folk Festival in Texas
Sitting on a blanket, meeting strangers
Full figure, long flowing lightweight dress, very pretty
Grew up in Birmingham, Alabama

ell, it's sort of like this: you get married in your mid-twenties and one day you wake up...after ten years or so, usually less, and you are bored. But then you probably have three or four kids and you don't want to make them grow up without their Daddy, so you find ways to entertain yourself. I took up photography and jazzercise. That filled up any spare time I had for a couple of years...then I asked Sam go to counseling with me. He was totally taken aback; he thought we had a great marriage. Maybe we did, I don't know because I've never believed anything the other wives said about their husbands or marriages. We were all out to impress each other with our kids or our money or our perfect sex lives and husbands. Or we lied about what a great relationship we had with our mothers and our kids.

I was just like everyone else in our neighborhood. I went to PTA when I couldn't avoid it, stuffed envelopes for the church fundraisers, and daydreamed about romance. I started reading romance novels and just knew that someday my romantic ideal would come. Boy was I surprised when he appeared in the body of my gay hairdresser. I started dying my hair jet black and wearing lots of black eye makeup as a way of acting out one of my romantic fantasies...I can't remember now if it was an Egyptian princess or Priscilla Presley, adored and desired by every man who saw me. So...along comes Mr. Tony. Oh my God! He just about fulfilled every romantic fantasy I had ever had. We chatted, we laughed. We had everything to talk about.

In the beginning all we did was shop together on Thursdays, his day off. Then he met my husband and children and they loved him. Sam did not feel threatened at all by Tony. After all, Tony was gay. Well, there is gay and then there's bisexual. I'm certain his first choice would have been men, but he had me. I would tell him these outrageous sexual fantasy stories that had been brewing in my head for years and he gleefully responded. One of my favorite stories was that I was a Love Goddess, the leader of an important religion and in order for him to get into the heavenly gates; he had to worship at my lower body. We loved being together making love as much as we loved shopping. Most of our days together ended with each of us screaming out these great orgasmic releases. My life was worth living. I knew that one day Tony would tell me to divorce Sam and that he would say I was the love of his life; he could never live without me.

This story has an altogether different ending than I had wished for. It was a Thursday. Sam called to ask me if I would like to go to lunch with him...a part of his new program of trying to pay more attention to me. I said I was sorry but I had already promised Tony that I would go with him to pick out wallpaper for his den. Sam sounded dejected.

It was about 2:30 p.m....Tony and I were in bed...we heard the knob turn on his front door. We stopped, frozen in time. We heard footsteps across the living room floor, coming towards the bedroom. I covered my head and made snoring noises. Tony jumped up and wrapped a towel around his waist. The door opened... and (with my head still covered) I heard Sam say, "Get out of that bed, Tammy Louise." I pulled the covers back, faked a yawn, and said, "Hi, sweetheart...oh my gosh! I must have slept for an hour. I was so tired and Tony said I could take a nap here in his bed." Then I got up, got dressed, chatted with both of them and left with Sam.

The incident was never mentioned. I changed my hair to red and now I dye it myself. Sam pays a lot more attention to me and Tony died last year in a car accident. Everybody figures out some way to survive and maybe my way wasn't the right one for anyone but me, but I'm not sorry at all and I would do it all over again, even the last day.

I would do that again too.

VANESSA

July 2, 2009
Houston, Texas
Hotel coffee Shop
Beautiful "chubby" girl...wide friendly face
with big brown eyes and easy laugh
Grew up in Beaumont, Texas

My name is Vanessa and I want to share my story. I will be fifty-five this year, am married, have had a radical mastectomy of my left breast, love my husband dearly, have six grown children and six grandchildren. This story is about religion. We both disliked religion as kids and when we were dating, only occasionally mentioned it. When we were married we picked a simple religion so that we could do something spiritual with the kids but I thought neither of us took it seriously; at least Victor said he was a free-thinker.

49

I was head over heels in love with my Victor. He is smart and paternal and accomplished in many sports and can play a variety of musical instruments and paints and draws and took good care of me with hot coffee and buttered toast on my bedside table each morning, helpful around the house and a great dad. I am an engineer and work for a large architectural firm where I have been for thirty years. They love me; pay me extremely well and I have a responsible position there. I get up each day, looking forward to going to the office.

My Victor is twelve years my senior and now retired. But this story doesn't start now and it certainly doesn't end now.

We had our kids one year apart, beginning when I was twenty-five. By the time I was thirty-one, I had six kids and was still breast feeding the last one. I made an appointment to have a tubal ligation, expecting Victor to be excited about having sex anywhere, anytime, without worrying about having more babies. He went nuts on me, acted like crazy person. I saw a side of him I did not know existed. He had not been raised to be religious and we had just sort of made up things as we went along...testing out what fit with our lifestyle.

So...imagine my surprise when he told me that if I got the tubal ligation there would be no more sex in this house for he believed sex was for making babies and if I was no longer willing or able to deliver a child, then we would not again engage in intercourse. What the hell was he talking about? I asked. Had he gone nuts? Granted, I was the one to initiate it most of the time but once he got started, he certainly wasn't repulsed by it by any means. I tried to talk with him, to reason with him but he was like a wall. I had the surgery and he moved into another room. At first I wept and felt sorry for myself but being resourceful and mad as hell, I decided I would just have to take my pleasure elsewhere. We continued with our marriage as if everything was just fine. The kids didn't seem to notice that dad slept in his study.

In June of the same year, I met Marshall. Married, he had no children, no sex in his marriage and no intention of getting a divorce. We started what played out to be the best relationship of my life. Even during the breast surgery and after...he was tender, caring, treated me as if I were the most precious thing on the planet. Not having a breast did not stop him at all from continuing to be a divine lover.

For eighteen years we have met twice a week at a charming little bed and breakfast just outside of our city. We are always happy to be together and reflecting on our history I think these are the reasons we have lasted so long: We agreed to never have jealousy over the spouse, never to call the other's house, never to expect divorce or marriage. We both knew what we wanted: respect, great sex, tenderness, conversation, laughter, and no promises for a future together. I believe life is about making choices that, without hurting others...(and, yes, it is your responsibility to keep your secrets to yourself) will improve the quality of your life.

From thirty-two until I was fifty we never missed a week, except of course, during the summer because of kids and vacations. Our lovemaking was playful, romantic, and adventuresome. The year I turned fifty, Marshall had his first heart attack. Guess I have failed to mention that he is a Type A personality and CEO of a large computer company. I was terrified. His secretary phoned me, but there was nothing I could do. I couldn't even visit the hospital for I would have revealed everything should I have encountered his wife. Not by words, but by my eyes and emotions.

I believe you can be in love with two persons at one time. I was in love with Marshall; even though I still loved Victor. So I went through six desperate months while Marshall healed. Then we resumed our meetings but each time he was fearful and cautious. He was no longer playful, but still romantic.

On a hot July day exactly one year later, he had another attack and this one was massive. This time I went to the hospital. I would sit in the waiting room until she was gone and then sneak up to his room. He was so weak; he could only give me a little smile and pat my hand. After he went back home it was months before I could see him. We met for breakfast and I barely recognized him. Thin and ashen, his hair and beard had turned snow white. We never made love again. He was too afraid. Slowly we drifted apart and last year he died in his sleep. I went to his funeral, stood in the back and wept silently behind my dark glasses.

NINA RUTH

August 1, 2007
Waco, Texas
Friend's home birthday party
Cute, too much: hair, boobs, boots, but very sweet
Grew up in Waco

I met him in a cowboy bar. I had just moved to Houston, didn't know anyone and decided it was time to learn to dance Western. He had the fairest skin I had ever seen, almost translucent, and had bright orange hair. We started kissing that night on the dance floor and Honey; he could kiss like a son-of-a-bitch! I would have kept going back just for those kisses even if we had not become such good friends. We decided immediately that we would not be lovers, just friends, just someone to hang out with and absolutely no sex. He is a very funny guy, always able to laugh at lame jokes and make fun of himself for being human.

53

We took a few weekend trips together to the Gulf. We were both fascinated by the tall ships that sometimes come into Galveston for repairs and we went to Galveston nearly every month. Every once in a while we might tease about one day doing "it" but at the same time promising never to fall in love. I had my list of requirements for a mate and he had his. At forty he had never been married and at forty-eight, I had been married far too many times to try it again. So we danced and laughed and talked a lot.

Then... one day... it was a cold, rainy Sunday in January and nothing to do if you were not a football fan... so I called Bernie. He answered in this fake Irish accent he used on Sundays. (On Mondays he was Mexican, Tuesday, Polish, etc.) I asked him if he wanted to do anything with me that afternoon. "Sure," he said. So what does he want to do? He replied that he wanted me to tie him up. "What do you mean, "tie you up?" "Just that. Tie me up." It is sort of like taking a dare...I'm a real sucker for a harmless dare.

So...after I had thought it over, I called him back and told him I would tie him up but that I didn't have any rope and he would have to meet me at Kroger and pay for the supplies I would need. A long silence at his end of the line and he said, "Now you won't hurt me, will you?" Of course he was half joking but still in shock that I had agreed to do this. We met at the store and he was in such a state of excitement he failed to notice just exactly what the supplies were. I bought ace bandages for his arms and legs, a nose plug, ear plugs, a scarf for a gag and one for a blindfold. We paid for our stuff and ran to the car in a rain so heavy it was coming down in sheets but Bernie didn't seem to notice because he was still trying to digest his good fortune.

We arrived back at his apartment where he made a fire and put on Etta James. Perfect. First he undressed and lay down spread eagle on the bed. He was taken aback when I explained that this was going to be total sensory deprivation, but he agreed to the program as I described it to him. What a great sport he was! It took me about fifteen minutes to get him all tied (not securely, just for the excitement of it all) and plugged and blindfolded. I completed the assignment...looked around the room to be certain I had not forgotten anything. Then I wrote a note, "Okay, I did it. You didn't tell me what to do next, so I guess I will just go on home." And I left. About an hour later he called me laughing so hard I thought he was going to swallow his tongue. At first he faked anger and then we laughed together.

I didn't see him for a month after that. He left a phone message that he had met someone whom he thought would be "the one". I listened to the machine over and over, each time realizing how much I had missed him, feeling sad and stupid for not realizing how much he meant to me before it was too late. Then I thought about the *LIST,* a lot of superficial requirements for becoming my partner in my next attempt at marriage. I found it, tore it into little pieces and flushed them.

I had never known anyone like Bernie before. He was real. He understood my foolishness...he could actually be childlike without being childish. We had the same stupid sense of humor. He was totally forgiving. He loved his Momma and Daddy. He liked cats. I phoned him and asked him to marry me. At first he thought this was a joke but when he realized I was not kidding he hung up the phone, came to my house, grabbed me and smothered me with kisses.

We have been blissfully happy for four years. Thanks, God. By the way, the other woman was never mentioned and sometimes I think he made her up just to bring me to my senses.

DEBORAH

August 21, 2009
Indianapolis, Indiana
Dental office waiting
Red hair, freckles, looks very young
Grew up in Indy

I was 10 when we moved to Indianapolis. I had never been out of the country and was awed by everything, especially the cute Italian boy whose family owned the corner grocery. His name was Angelo. His eyes were big and brown and he was fifteen. And he didn't look twice at me. Until five years later. The Italian kids in our neighborhood didn't play with the other kids. Not because they didn't want to, but because their parents would get very mad when they were caught out late at night playing kick the can with us, or just hanging underneath the street light.

We didn't do anything that they didn't do, it was a simple, typical fifties life then. But the south side of Indianapolis was pretty much owned by big Italian Catholic families and the only reason we even lived there was because they also were slum lords and owned old rent houses that our parents had to live in because we had not been in the city it long enough to establish bank accounts or credit or references which would allow us to move into nicer neighborhoods.

Angelo's dad ran a grocery for everyone on our street, charging our folks three times what they would pay at Kroger or Safeway. Half the time my dad was out of work, because his union was on strike, so we stayed in debt to the Marino family.

By the time I was fifteen, I was a beauty. I can say that now because I am no longer hung up on being modest about how I looked back then. I excelled at everything in school and could outrun any boy or girl in our neighborhood because I had legs that were long and strong and beautiful. I had thick, blonde hair which I wore in one braid because I was more interested in athletics than style. In spite of all that, I still became a shimmering glob of protoplasm whenever I caught a glimpse of Angelo. He was in college at Notre Dame but came home most weekends to work for his family. The fall I was fifteen, he actually said hello to me. I had to go home and lie down.

The Christmas vacation when I was fifteen and Angelo was twenty, he came back to the neighborhood to work in the store. His dad was sick and the brothers were all too young to take care of the accounting and stocking. My grandmother was the only one to know of my crush on Angelo and her advice was, "go down there and make friends with his mother. But don't even look once at him or she will know."

For the next three weeks I carried out Grandma's plan for making Sophia like me. I made myself useful. She didn't have a daughter and she fell for me. So did Angelo. Sophia pretended not to notice but she found occasions to send the two of us in her car to run errands. And she invited me to dinner a couple of times until Vinnie got out of the hospital. In January, Angelo went back to school. We wrote letters every week until spring break. He came home for a month and went back to work in the store. Sophia had resumed her stay-at-home mom status because Vinnie was back to take care of the businesses. Occasionally Sophia had called me to visit her for lunch, but the calls had become less and less frequent and after Angelo came home, she stopped calling me.

One night when we were going to get supper, I suggested we go to Alfredo's...a neighborhood Italian place that both of our families frequented. Angelo hesitated, and then he said, "We can't go there."

"Why?" I didn't understand his response. He looked at me for a long time and then, "I can't be seen with you there. I can't let my dad know we're dating."

"We are not just dating, Angelo, we are in love."

"I am so in love with you, but you know how my dad would feel about my dating anyone who is not Italian."

"So, I'm not good enough for you?" I began to cry.

"It's not that, it's just a cultural thing. We're a family. A special kind of family and they would never let me marry you."

I got out of his car and walked back to my house. Spring came and went, and I cried for him every night. In June I decided to go to summer school so that I could graduate at sixteen and go away. He graduated from college that summer and never came back to work for his father. He went to Chicago for graduate school and then moved to Los Angeles. I went to college in Ohio and married a nice boy named Clint just after we graduated. It was 1969 and I was twenty years old.

By 1985 I was divorced with children almost grown and I got homesick for Indianapolis and moved back there. Just a few months after my return, my Grandma called to tell me that Angelo's mother had died. Even though Grandma had always felt sad and responsible for having encouraged me to fall in love with Angelo, once again, she pushed me to him. "I think you should go to the funeral," she said, "Just to represent our family."

The funeral home was arranged in a semi-circle, with the casket just in front of the center section. Angelo was in the last seat of the front row and he saw me as I went in to take my seat. Our eyes met. My heart stopped. The service was about to begin but he came to me, put his arms around me, and said, "Oh, Deborah, my beautiful Deborah." I didn't go to the grave site, but went back to Grandma's house.

Just as it was getting dark, he came there for me. He had never married. He said everything I needed to hear. He asked me to marry him. We've had almost 20 years of joyous life together. He says he knew we would be together if he waited long enough.

BETTE EPSTEIN

EMMALOU

February 11, 2007
Dallas, Texas
Le Madeleine Café
Very sexy, long legs, long hair, dark skin
Grew up in Dallas

don't think Terri ever really loved me. I was her first lesbian affair and she was 40, for God's sake. It would seem if she had really been gay, it would have come out before then. I've known all of my life that I love women. When I was five, I had a best friend named Hillary. She lived down the street and she was crazy about me and would do anything I asked her to. One day we were playing house and she was the husband. She asked me if I wanted her to kiss me "down there" like she had seen her dad do to her mom one day when they thought she was asleep. I said, "Sure." We stayed "best friends" throughout high school, dated boys, and kept our parents happy for a very long time because they suspected nothing.

Years later my Daddy, the pillar of our small community in New Mexico, made a deal with me that if I got "straightened out" he would send me to Europe for the summer. During the first session with the therapist, she asked me to go back to my first homosexual affair. Hillary's face smiled back at me.

Anyway, Terri is far more butch-looking than I am and I took one look at her and just figured she knew. We are both parole officers and that Lew Sterrett building is full of gay women. So I asked her for a date. She looked at me sort of puzzled at first but she accepted. I didn't try to kiss her or hold her hand for a month and she didn't act as if she expected me to. We went to concerts, the Symphony, roller-blading at White Rock, and out for long dinners. I even took her home to meet my folks.

The first time we made love it was in Taos in December. The light snow falling on her skin made her look like a chocolate chip cookie with white sprinkles. I told her so and she slapped my arm, laughed at me, and said I was actually a little light for her. We continued to flirt throughout dinner. The restaurant was a collection of small rooms, each with its own chiminea burning something with a heavy sandalwood fragrance. I drank hazelnut coffee that night for the first time. We began those tender little kissy-face kisses there in the restaurant and by the time we were back in our hotel room we rushed into lovemaking.

By morning there were no parts at each other that we had not explored and she was even more eager and aggressive than I was. We continued to do the same social things back at home as before, only now we added dancing and holding hands in public. I met her family and they didn't question our sleeping together in their home in Oklahoma. On her birthday the next year, we exchanged rings which we wore on our left hands. We planned the honeymoon in Germany that fall and started a joint savings for it. The trip was incredible and when we returned, we moved in together.

Then it became wrong. Terri became distant and fixed up the guest room for herself. She stopped being physical, wouldn't even kiss or hold me. A little bit at a time she started packing up her stuff, thinking I wouldn't notice. Lots of night I cried myself to sleep but I was afraid to ask. I couldn't ask if she was leaving, I wanted to stay in denial with my hopes.

She came into the kitchen that morning and sat across the table from me, holding my hand. "It's not right for me, Emma." I asked her if it was the woman/woman thing.

"The best thing I can do is to tell you, it's as if I've dared to do something wonderful and exciting and lived to tell about it and now I just want to go home."

I asked her if she ever really loved me...had she ever been IN love with me. She just looked at me for the longest time and then stood up, threw her backpack over her shoulder and left.

BETTE EPSTEIN

LOLA

March 30, 2008
Barnes & Nobel Bookstore
San Antonio, Texas
Eccentric, interesting, nice
Grew up in Arkansas

*A*s I share this great love with you, please try to avoid making assumptions. I was twenty years his senior but he was never my boy-toy and I was never his Jocasta. We were lovers, pure and simple, we were lovers. He was eighteen when he left Dothan, Alabama, and moved here to Jackson; fresh out of high school and looking for a way to make a living and attend the art school where I worked. I saw him in the hallway just outside the dance studio the first day he was here. Michelangelo's David, that's who he was, a cap of blonde curls cascading to his broad shoulders, flat tanned

67

stomach. My mouth dropped open and he caught me staring at him. Big, friendly smile he gave me.

I walked over to him and reached out my hand, "Hi, I'm Lola. I work here." "Rafe, I want to go to school here." We walked outside together, went for coffee, stayed up till midnight at my house, talking.

He was one of ten kids of a factory worker and a mom who worked in the school cafeteria. He couldn't wait to leave his small town. No money, no friends, no job but miles and miles of talent. He was staying in a boarding house (yes, we still had boarding houses in Jackson in 1981) near my place and the next day I saw his portfolio. I instantly made a decision to make him my project and before the month was over he was enrolled, had a student loan, a job, and had moved in with me.

The first month, we just got to know each other, being tender and curious. The second month, we began sleeping in the same bed. By the end of the third month, we were lovers. He was a virgin. I was not only thirty-eight; I had been married twice and had slept with probably thirty men. It was the times and I was a free spirit. I taught him everything I knew and it wasn't enough. We bought books. We learned massage. We took Yoga. My friends loved him. This grand and glorious affair lasted in its perfection exactly five years.

On Rafe's twenty-third birthday he told me he was gay. I didn't blink. I don't know if I suspected all along or if I just knew I couldn't do anything about it. So, all I could say was, "...and your point?" I guess I started to cry for he held me then. Held me and we made love. We continued to make love until Leonard came along and after that was over; we went back to making love as if he had never told me.

Then there was Sam and Oscar and Jack. We continued to live together and for a while Jack lived with us...until he died. AIDS was sort of new to us then. We knew about it. Everyone talked about it...but no one believed it would ever come into their lives. We were the beautiful, artistic, "in" crowd in Jackson.

We were invited to just about every social event because I was well known for my paintings and Rafe was fast becoming a high-priced sculptor. Folks loved to watch us dance at these events for Rafe was a marvelous dancer and we were both tall and thin and he would sweep me across the dance floor as if we were skating. Both vain, we enjoyed being the center of attention. We were so smug. I truly believed Rafe would "grow out of it" and come back to me. I haven't mentioned how broken my heart was the first time I saw him with a man; haven't told you how I threw up for days.

But I loved that man with every cell of my body. HE WAS ME! I was carved from his soul. Many times he came home from being with a man, crawled into our bed, held onto me and cried himself to sleep. Often I would see him sitting in the dark, knees pulled up to his chest, rocking back and forth and saying over and over, "I hate being fucking gay!"

Our lives went on pretty much like that for fifteen years, even though in 1987, Rafe was diagnosed with HIV. He stayed symptom free until 1998. We kept it our secret. He was aware of how to protect his partners and did and was never promiscuous after he knew. By '98, every serious art collector in Jackson and Birmingham and Atlanta owned at least one of his sculptures. His energy soared those ten years and he turned out one marvelous piece after another...like a man possessed. And, of course, he was.

In September 1998, Rafe became ill and died in December. I was in the bed holding him when he released his last breath. As if he felt the pain was a purging of his sins and of those demons who had haunted him all of his life, he refused any medication. Just before he left, he looked at me and said, "I'm sorry Sweetheart. I never meant to hurt you." He really loved me, you know. Nature just fucked us up.

OLIVIA

June 2, 1999
Atlanta, Georgia
UFO club Meeting
Beautiful, like 20's French film star
Grew up in Dallas

*I*f you ask me, all religion is good for is fucking things up. I am not talking about God, goddammit; I'm talking about fucking religion. About all those pious tight-asses, who are nothing but small potato politicians running the churches, the synagogues, and the mosques? The Pope telling people they have to keep having babies so they will send more money to the church — and then telling the young men who become priests that they can never have sex — that they will fry in the lake of fire if they hug a woman and get a hard-on. Religion messed with my life in too many ways!

I was twenty-six that summer. I can't even remember the year, sometime in the Fifties or Sixties — well, must have been the Fifties. My ex-husband, the father of my three children, had been Catholic. My first mistake: believing him when he told me he wasn't really into it, but he wanted his folks to like me so I had to promise to raise the kids as Catholics and get married in the church. I did all of that. He didn't lie; he really didn't care about being a Catholic —until the next wife wanted to also get married in the church.

Once we got married it was bam, bam, bam — just like that, a new baby every year. But, ah, I was in love. I would have given him anything he wanted. We married the day after I graduated from high school and by twenty-two; I had three kids and a traveling salesman for a husband. Imagine my surprise when I received divorce papers from his attorney while he was out of town. I ended up in Beverly Hills Sanitarium for three months of shock and insulin treatments, trying to get me back into my body.

Mother was still caring for the babies when I returned from the hospital. It was three weeks later when the priest came to visit me. He felt my anger; saw my rage when I slammed the door in his face. Determined, he came back again and again until finally I let him in. He was well over 6 feet tall, blond, blue-eyed, and the most pleasant face I have ever seen. I trusted him. I invited him to sit down and served coffee. He explained that he had come at the request of Harold's family; that they wanted me to agree to an annulment of our marriage.

I almost turned the table over I was so enraged. We had three children. Did he expect this priest or the Pope to think our marriage was never consummated? I screamed this at the priest. He didn't flinch. He didn't disagree with me either, just kept that stupid neutral look on his face while I pounded my fist into the wall. The next day he came back and I decided to play it to the hilt. Now, in my defense, you may need to realize I was still mental when this all began. I purposely seduced him. First I acted the innocent, pitiful, rejected housewife. Then I began dressing in a more revealing way and speaking soft and whispery and touching his hand or his arm or his shoulder when I made a point.

Soon he would hug me hello and goodbye. One day I dared him to take off his collar so that he could see what he would look like as a regular man. We closed the front door and drapes and he did just that. He was beautiful. I put my arms around his neck to help him loosen the collar and when I breathed his scent I knew this was no longer an act. I really wanted this man. Harold's family began putting more and more pressure on me for the annulment but I held off for I knew that when I gave it, Father Paul would not come back.

He did not rush me for a decision. As the weeks passed, we developed a routine. He would come in, lock the front door, close the drapes and remove his collar. Then we would hug for a very long time. But no kisses — yet.

It was early December and I knew the children would be coming back to live with me soon and so I put up the Christmas tree early. I built a fire, turned on the twinkling lights, and set a romantic stage for our meeting that Friday. I remembered that he only ate fish on Friday and so I prepared dinner and lit the candles. The snow flurries had turned to rain that afternoon and when he came in, his jacket was wet. I helped him remove it, noticing that his shirt was also soaked. "Wait a minute, Father Paul; I have something you can put on."

I liked calling him Father; somehow it made the whole thing seem more daring. I brought out one of Asshole's flannel shirts he had left there and Paul slipped his arms into it. The sleeves were much too long for him, so I gently helped him roll them up. Our eyes met. He reached down and picked me up and I wrapped my legs around his waist real tight and he kissed me hard and passionately. He carried me to the bedroom, gently undressed me, and covered me while he slipped out of his clothes. Then he did a funny thing — he crossed himself before he moved into bed with me. I giggled. He, realizing the humor of his actions, giggled with me. I had never been with a big man before and I must tell you, there is something to it. I came like a woman deprived, screaming out every thrill, every delight, every surge of blood as it released to go back into my body. I felt sorry for any woman who had never been made love to by this man.

Dinner was long forgotten for we were far hungrier for love than food. He left at noon the next day and that was the beginning of a love affair that lasted two years. I gave Asshole the annulment and started going to Mass just so I could look at Paul when he was serving God. Sometimes I felt real bad about what we were doing and sometimes I just said, "To hell with it." We were so in love. There was no part of him I didn't like; he was just the ultimate human.

The church found out. There was a transfer to Detroit with a warning that if there was ever another hint of scandal, he would be defrocked. He loved me so much he left the church. But, ultimately...I guess he loved God more than me. Six months later he lay down on the Davenport one rainy Sunday afternoon and never opened his eyes again.

There were tears on the pillow by his face. He was thirty-nine and had no history of illness. He just died of a broken heart. I was put back into Beverly Hills Sanitarium and this time I stayed there for six months. Nothing helped. I left my kids with my mother again and just wandered around for a long time until I could safely go back into our home without screaming. Even though I hate religion, I believe in souls and I believe Paul is the other half of mine. I'm seventy-eight now and I've had two more husbands but there has never been a day in my life when I didn't think of him and ache for his arms around me.

BETTE EPSTEIN

MISHEY

Pasadena, California
Unity Church Meditation
Waiting for the rain to stop so we could walk the labyrinth

He is getting married tomorrow. At twilight, in his sisters backyard, under a chuppah made from bamboo and silk sheets tied up with satin ribbon and fresh roses. I'm invited. No, I won't be going. There will be lily pods floating among the candles in the pool and Japanese lanterns hanging from all the trees. Violinists will be strolling the first hour while everyone has cocktails and they wait for the bride to appear to have her veil lifted so he can identify her as the woman he has chosen. How can he say yes to the wrong woman?

I drove past the house today and looked into the yard. It is magnificent. Over three hundred guests will be there, all wearing white. Even the Rabbi will be in white. No, I don't want to marry him. Never did, even when we were madly in love. When he told me he was going to ask Rachel to marry him, I broke down and cried and asked, "But what about us? What will happen to us? Me and you, Eli? What will happen to Mishey and Eli? "

He held me and tried to find words to comfort me. He just didn't get it. He really believed that we will be able to still be friends and do the things together that we have always done. In ten years he has not missed a gathering of my family, never had a birthday that we didn't give him a surprise party. We have gone all over the country to see our favorite bands, to Museum openings and he even indulged my fascination with dog shows.

My mom told me I needed to make friends with Rachel, become her best buddy, and invite her to our family events along with Eli. I did that. She was cool with our friendship and even became friends with my siblings and parents. She is an awesome woman but she's not me. Eli and I started dating in high school, stayed close during college, dated again in graduate school (his, I chose to be a free spirit artist and designer).

By our mid 20's we were madly in love again and started talking about a life together with kids and cats and dogs and maybe even a parrot. It sounded like what I wanted. I certainly wanted Eli. There was only one tiny difference; Eli wanted a religious woman. Not Orthodox or even close, but someone who would enjoy services each week and getting involved in the activities there. My family is Conservative (our Rabbi says that is a code word for Cafeteria, we take the part we like and leave the rest).and sort of three times a year Jewish. That's not quite true but it's never going to be my life. Eli never mentioned much about religion until we started talking about kids. I just figured, if we're both Jewish, we're both Jewish.

We could have fun in a crowd or just the two of us because he is the most clever, witty, best storytelling guy you will meet and I was always his best audience. We loved the same things, adventuresome things even we are both kind of nerdy, not athletic looking people. For his 21st birthday, we went sky-diving, the next year we did hang-gliding. We rock climb, scuba dive, and we both are voracious readers. We love books, not electronic books, but real paper that you can feel and smell. I'm telling you, we are meant for each other. So how did this great love go south? Well, I don't think it did. I believe he is still in love with me, but he found someone else while I was finding myself. It was three summers ago. Eli and I had decided to marry on our 28th birthday (yes, we have the same birthday and 28 is some astrological special day), which would be in 18 months.

That's when I left for Mexico, then Thailand, and Belize, and South Africa. Now I wasn't just slacking. I had cashed in an old insurance settlement check from a car accident when I was fifteen. And, I wasn't vacationing. I took a course in something in every country I visited. I took painting, sculpting, silver-smithing, fiber arts and many day courses in other little cities near where I was staying.

The fun I had during those months just gave me more of a sense that marriage was not for me. I made friends everywhere, danced and drank and laughed and had absolutely no one to please except myself. Every day after school in every exotic place I lived, I met friends for some other activities. We took lots of dance classes, I learned to play the guitar a little bit, even took a songwriting class. I sometimes forgot to be at the appointed place when Eli was going to call. I didn't fall in love with anyone else, but there may have been a few flirtations and crushes. I was just being free and excited about my life.

Eli met me at the airport and took me immediately to his new apartment. He had dinner prepared and ready to warm up. We lit the fireplace logs, drank wine, made love and then I felt flat. I couldn't tell if it was me or Eli. I got a sense that another spirit had entered our world. Eighteen is a magical number and in all that time, I didn't expect Eli to live those months alone, but something was definitely amiss. He came to my folk's home the following night and after everyone had drifted off, we were sitting in the porch swing when he asked me. "Do you still want to marry me?"

"Of course I do."

It was too late. Although I felt I had hesitated only for a brief moment, it was long enough for him to feel the hesitation and feel my fear. I looked into his eyes and we both cried. I love that man with all my heart and have not even come close to loving anyone else. But I don't want a traditional marriage with kids and dogs and religion. I want to see the world and not ever feel obligated to call home to reassure someone of my love. Is that narcissistic or hedonistic? I don't know. Since we have the same birthday, it can't be astrological.

"You're a free spirit, Mishey. You want to fly and have adventures even without me. I don't want to do much of anything without you."

I begged him to give me another chance. We spent the next six months being the same as we had been before I left but there was always this elephant in the room. I thought it was me...all me. But as time came closer to when we had to plan a wedding, Eli had the talk with me.

"I would never have noticed her if the Mishey who took off to see the world had come back the same girl. You know I want a simple life right here in Pasadena. I can't have that with you. I can have it with Rachel".

I made the right decision but I hate the fact that I couldn't trust myself to go to the wedding and not make a scene. I kept having this fantasy. At the end of the ceremony, just before Eli was to break the glass....I stand up and yell, "What about us, Eli...? What about you and Mishey?....I love youuuuu!"

BETTE EPSTEIN

MIRIAM

February, 2001
Kansas City, Missouri
Class on swing dancing, coffee later
Very childlike, dresses like a little girl
Grew up in St. Louis

My father was a lot older than most dads when I was born. He was sixty-two and although there were a lot of things he didn't do with me, (things I believe to be unimportant like playing tennis, roller skating, Frisbee, etc.). I always felt precious when he was near me. I was thirty-five when Daddy died, so he lived a very long and full life.

My first husband was about my age. Not the most handsome boy on the block, but he had a way with words that certainly made him the most charming. I was swept away by his stories and laughter. We were together for about 10 years when I finally realized and admitted that he had probably slept with everyone on our block. I forgave him and he went for therapy...we went for therapy...the whole block went for therapy, pretty much.

We stayed together another five years after my realization and the therapy did me a world of good. I discovered I needed to feel precious. I needed to be remembered on special occasions and have my coffee brought to me in bed once in a while. Those things had seemed so shallow to me when I was trying to be the perfect wife to the perfect husband. He didn't understand precious. He didn't understand why I was not thrilled with a birthday gift he brought to me because his secretary reminded him to. We divorced.

After a slow start, my life moved on. I dated and even got engaged once but each time I realized I had assumed the role of making the other person feel precious, thinking he would see how I wanted to be loved...and do it.

It was February 1991. I had gone to a lecture on spirituality at our Unity Church. The speaker was a man who had written a number of books on finding your bliss using yoga. I couldn't take my eyes off him. He had a slight build, wizened face, and the countenance of an angel. He was signing books after his talk and I timidly went up to him to make a purchase. He took my hand and kissed it, looked deep into my eyes, and asked me to meet him for coffee later. He was obviously more than twenty years my senior but I swear, I can't remember noticing.

There I was, once again, swept away by a man's charm. This time it was with a man of many years but with the spirit of a teenager. We dated. We became lovers. Sean had the skills and stamina of a man half his age. He was a master of Tantric Yoga and knew exactly how to apply this discipline. No, I did not replace my Daddy with Sean. I simply knew, on some deep level, what I needed in a mate. The fact he is, actually, almost thirty years my senior, is of no consequence. I believed I could have been happy with a man my own age or even younger if I had found one who knew how to love me as I needed to be loved.

God willing, we will have a lot of satisfying years together.

TALINA

August 21, 2009
Starbucks
Bowling Green, Kentucky
Grew up in Nashville

The voice mail on my answering machine plays, "At Last My Love Has Come Along".....and I mean that with all my heart. I was 50 when I met Evan three years ago and even though I had been married three times already, this is the love of my life.

I grew up in a normal enough family, six kids, and parents who worked hard and didn't put much pressure on us to be over-achievers even though we were smarter than most. My brother, Jason, and I were only fourteen months apart and from the first time I was aware of my big brother, I couldn't get enough of him. He was funny, clever, poetic, musical, and could do an impersonation of most of the celebrities we saw on television.   We were each other's best friends and he treated me like big brothers in the old classics treated their little sisters. He was always very protective of me, praised me and took me on adventures in this city that most kids growing up in the 60's never knew existed.

Many Sundays when we were not yet full-blown teens, we would take a city bus downtown, get a transfer and go to the end of that line, get off the bus there and explore the neighborhood where we got off. Then we would catch the late afternoon bus back to downtown, get another transfer and go home. Because of his fearlessness and curiosity, we would sometimes explore the sewer lines under the city by crawling down into a manhole and walking through those tunnels until either I got scared or nasty or just plain bored. We figured out how to sneak into most of the movie houses and there was not a movie shown the year I was 14 that we didn't see. We were what is now called dumpster divers and compiled quite a collection of "treasures" that Mom and Dad would eliminate once it got too big. Growing up did not stop our being companions.

When Jason was 26 he got married, had a great job, and moved his new bride into the same building where he and I had shared an apartment. That was cool, she liked me. A couple of years later, I married for the first time to Forrest. He was okay with the relationship I had with my brother, but when he got a job promotion and transfer to another city, I wouldn't go with him. My next husband, Roger, was just not a good choice for me for he did not have family and didn't understand the closeness of mine.   Playing table games on Friday nights with your siblings and parents was not his idea of a good time and since he was not creative enough to offer us an alternative, we eventually drifted apart.   By our mid-thirties Jason began to get fat, and with that he eventually became diabetic.

His wife, Susan, and I did a bad thing; we spoiled him something awful.   He let us.   And he got fatter and fatter and more unable to do things for himself.   I moved in with them.   Then I married Roy and we took a place nearby. The four of us had fun for a long time until Jason's health became our total focus. I am a school-teacher so I was home by four and at that time, Susan would go to her work as a parole officer. We juggled work and Jason and a little bit of fun for a few years and when Roy finally got tired of that life and left.   Susan, Jason and I bought a house together in the inner-city.   There had never been time or an inclination for any of us to have children because Jason was our child.

I guess it was six years ago when Susan seemed to just get up one day and began to pack her personal stuff. Jason and I were totally blindsided by her actions. As she put the last box by the front door, she looked at me and said, "I'm sorry. I do love you." And then she put her arms around Jason and hugged his 400 pound body as tightly as she could. "I may regret this every day for the rest of my life, but I will die young if I stay here. I just didn't get the caretaker gene. Please don't hate me". We still see her sometimes and she and Jason stayed in love for the rest of his life.

A year after Susan left, Jason had gained another fifty pounds and developed a boil-like eruption, which would not heal, on his left leg. After a lot of surgeries to save the leg, three years ago, it had to be taken off just below the knee. We cried and cried together for a few weeks and then we began to heal. Our humor came back and life looked pretty good; Jason even stopped eating so much and began to lose weight.

Three years ago the man who had mowed the yard for me just stopped coming by. The lawn had begun to look pretty terrible and one day I was standing out on the front porch, looking at the weeds sprouting up everywhere, when I heard a male voice say, "If you have a mower, I can take care of that for you". I turned around to see a very handsome young man standing behind me, smiling. He said his name was Max and that he worked for a number of my neighbors. I didn't even ask for a reference for his charm swept me away. When he was finished with the yard work I invited him in to pay him and to meet Jason. They were immediately infatuated with each other and shared a lot of the same interests, taste in music, liberal politics and Max loved jigsaw puzzles as we did. The downside of this new friendship was that Max lived in a halfway house nearby because he was a recovering alcoholic and he still needed a support group. I told Jason that we needed to do a background check on this new friend, but Jason would not hear of it. "I can tell all I know about a person by my intuition".

Max was a small man but strong as any weightlifter. He quickly took over all of the care of Jason

His baths, getting him into and out of the wheelchair, practice walking on his prosthesis, and he built the most elaborate ramp from the house to the car that I have ever seen. We three spent almost all of our time together and seldom stopped laughing. Six months later, Max moved into our house. At first I was a little jealous of his friendship with Jason but Jason never failed to include me in every project, every conversation and when they went to a film or out to dinner together, I was always invited but allowed Jason to find some "guy" time with his new friend.

Having Max in our lives allowed us to do the things we had loved so much in the past but were not mobile enough to do them because I was just not strong enough to maneuver the wheelchair. We started once again to go to the Art Museum, to the Arboretum for concerts in the evenings, and to the parks for cookouts on Sunday afternoons. Often Susan would join us and it felt like two couples doing regular couple stuff. She and Jason would hold hands and whisper quietly together. Once when it was obvious they wanted to be alone, Max took my hand and suggested we take a walk by the ponds nearby. He didn't let go of my hand and there was such an electricity there that my fingers actually tingled. Without saying a word, we both knew we were in love.

We didn't talk about our feelings to each other or to Jason. It was as if it had to be kept this big secret. But Jason quickly picked up on it and began asking the two of us to run errands for him, to go out at night so he could have some "alone time." And I could feel his emotions swell when he would think he had seen a spark between us.

At Thanksgiving two years ago we went to Mom's house and there, among all of our siblings, Max stood up and made an announcement. "I'm probably here because of my friendship with Jason but what Jason and Talina both know, but would never talk about with me or you, until now, is that I am in love with your sister and I hope she will marry me", and then "for if she won't marry me, then I'm going to have to marry Jason!"

Everyone laughed and immediately embraced this strange little man. Of course I said yes. We still have not had a marriage ceremony. On Christmas day right after Max asked me to marry him, Jason somehow stepped on something sharp and made a cut on his foot. I began taking him to a wound specialist for treatment. The treatment went on for six weeks without a healing. Max and I put him into the hospital where he continued treatment for another six weeks. He was released and sent home. I didn't tell him but of course he knew that there was no healing to be had in that foot and he would soon have to give it up to surgery, leaving him permanently confined to the chair.

Seven days after returning home from the hospital, Jason died in his sleep. I feel he willed it. He could not bear the thought of being a double amputee and at the mercy of caregivers completely.

I feel Jason would have done whatever he had to do if he thought he would be crossing over and leaving me alone but he knew he could go on now. Maybe his angels brought Max to us. Or maybe Max is our angel. Jason and I were born to be together as sure as if we had been twins attached at the heart, for we were. We loved the same things, the same world, and the same people. This story was meant to be about my loving Max, but that never would have happened if I had not loved Jason first.

Yes, my love has come along and this time it brings romance and love making and long walks.

KALI

May 22, 2009
Indianapolis, Indiana.
Conference on Health
Unique, Eurasian, sexy
Grew up in Ohio

*I*t was 1992. I had been invited by a best friend to participate in a Healing Arts Exchange Program in Kiev, Ukraine. A few months prior to that, I had been hurt to the core of my being, leaving a gaping hole in my emotional heart, by a longtime love who decided to leave L.A., where we had shared a home for 5 years. He told me the move back to his hometown would be temporary, but when I returned from work on the day of his leaving, I discovered he had taken everything that could remotely be considered his own. I was still healing and a romance was the farthest thing from my thinking.

In my opinion the airport personnel in Kiev weren't excited about 14 Americans coming into their country, except, perhaps, for the officers on duty who insisted on collecting an additional $50 for the "updated" visas we had to purchase at the airport. I won't even talk about the flight there from Brussels. After a several hour wait we were finally greeted by the director of the program, and more money exchanged hands. We were not told there was another $100 for the host families who would provide for us during our stay in Kiev.

I was tired, mad and ready to go home. Thinking I could count on my three good friends on the trip for comic relief, I quickly realized I would be totally separated from Eve, Aiden and Dan. I was on the verge of tears.

Feeling like quadruplets separated at birth, we were placed on buses that would take each of us to our designated homes. As the bus pulled out we were introduced to Miguel who was dressed very upper middle class and I wondered how he had been privileged to be so elegant, his designer watch, elegant trousers and shirt, but, oh, the beige shiny shoes had to go. He looked late 30"s and had eyes so brilliant that he put on a light show. Well, maybe just for me. Later Eve told me she thought he looked like white bread and mayonnaise from Alabama. He was one of the organizers of this journey and would be our director now that we were here.

When the bus came to the stop where my host family lived, it took several men, Miguel included, carrying the bags filled with gallons of drinking water, up the stairs.

He didn't complain, just gave me a big smile. We were to all meet the next morning for a tour of the city and lunch.

My curiosity about Miguel continued the next day when we were given the best seats at the restaurant (Eve, Aiden, Dan and I are all vegetarians, a daunting task for a Kiev chef.) Miguel was served a plate piled high with various mystery meats which he quickly devoured. Why was he treated so well?

The next day and every day, Miguel and I did not take our eyes off each other. He introduced me to the students on day one with what I assumed to be a very detailed description of my work for my little room in the science hall had to be scrapped to accommodate the overflow crowd which grew every day. After a flirtation that grew more intense during days three, four and five, he finally invited me to lunch. On day six he invited me to meet his wife and have dinner at their home. WIFE??? I was devastated. But, I accepted the invitation. I liked Valya, a beautiful woman eleven years his senior but ageless in appearance, immediately, but grew even more confused as he was continuing to be affectionate and flirtatious with me. She, also, was affectionate to me. This is not Los Angeles behavior!

The following day we were to leave Kiev and go to Cherkassy for the final week of the tour and I had to be at the shore for the hydroplane early the next morning. Suddenly Miguel put on his coat and indicated to his sweet wife that he would be home late, but not to worry. It had gotten chilly and there was a heavy downpour. Miguel hugged me close to him as we waited for a taxi. All the way home he kissed me gently on the lips. I'm sure even the taxi driver thought this strange behavior for an even stranger couple.

On the hydroplane to Cherkassy, Miguel sat across from me, never taking his eyes from me. Once he even hugged my knees! He had this thing for knees I discovered later.

When we arrived at my host family, Miguel hung out for a couple of hours. The next day he took me to my translator for dinner and each time she left the room he would jump next to me. When we left her apartment we had sex in the hallway and it was so awful it almost killed the feeling I had for him. But...When he left the next day to return to Kiev, I was terribly lonesome for him. I told Eve about the sex and she was totally disgusted. "You always go for those pasty little white men with shiny shoes." Her judgment brought me back to reality and I felt for just one brief moment that my feelings for Miguel and his for me, was turning into a sleazy romance novel. That was not what I wanted at all.

On the 3rd day in Cherkassy, after I dragged my tired ass up the stairs to my host home, the door swung open and it was Miguel. Lola had invited him to stay and provided a private room. She had figured it out, of course. It was marvelous and we fell in love. We continued to see each other for the next four days and our feelings grew so strong that we stopped talking; all we did was sit close and hold hands. He's married!!! Would I want someone to do this with MY husband...these thoughts would not leave me. But...the depth of our love didn't leave me either. I didn't want it to end.

You may be thinking I was just overwhelmed by the breakup with Jim and the sensations of being a "rock star healer" from the U.S...adored by so many...or the excitement of sneaking around, hiding our love from the others. Once when I saw Aiden he said to me, "Why are you working so hard...we seldom see you."

Eve had made everyone mad when she slipped away two days early from Cherkassy because she had grown so attached to her host family in Kiev and did not want to go back home without seeing them again. She found a photographer who offered to take her back on a bus with him if she would assist him in a wedding shoot. I thought she had abandoned me, but in an angry voice she reminded me that I had eyes for no one but Miguel this entire week. And she was right.

On the hydroplane Miguel and I could not even sit close to each other and back in Kiev at the airport I thought my heart would break from longing. Too many people around for any serious displays of affection and so we had to be circumspect in our behavior.

On the interminable trip back to the states, I was so annoyed with Eve and the others talking, talking, talking...and Eve constantly doing these damned stretches. I didn't want to be distracted from my sweet memories. Home again in Los Angeles, I signed onto the internet and there was Miguel. We talked a few times each day.

After a few months, Miguel was divorced, but not because of me. It seemed her being his senior had started to be an issue for Valya and she became very insecure and decided to divorce him. Of course, there is the possibility that a lot more was in play in that scenario than just her age. She was not a stupid woman.

I returned with a different group in '96. It was awkward at first, for both of us but more for him. He arranged for me to stay with a friend of his because he was not yet comfortable taking me to his new apartment. But one day we did go to his place and we made love in a tiny chair. He was so exhilarated by it that he danced and sang all around the room. (I have a picture of that!) And that was the day I realized he was tone deaf because the sounds coming from his throat were agony, not music...which, actually, only made me love him more.

Geography played the biggest part in ending our love affair. Kiev is sooo far from Los Angeles and although he has a lot more money than most of the recent capitalists there, he still had a lot of responsibility at home and frequent travel was not possible. Not often enough to satisfy the needs of adults, who hunger for affection from each other, anyway. The words he spoke to me, the tenderness of his touch, and the lights in his eyes when he saw me....It was as if he became the healer and I the one who needed to be healed. I got over my former love far more quickly than I ever imagined.

Miguel will always be in my romantic heart. This love affair will have a special place in the journal of my journey through life.   Wherever you are my sweet Miguel…I hope you see this story and know I often fall asleep in your arms.

VERONICA

Today... October 10, 2011
Age unknown, tallish, slender
Grew up in Indiana

S o I always knew a real cute boy would fall in love with me someday. Well, I didn't really, but I hoped he would. I was a romantic. I read Love Comics and anything that had a happy ending; I would lie in bed at night and imagine what he would look like. This all started when I was about twelve.

It seemed to take forever for him to get there. I was out of high school before I first saw him. It was at a dance at the army base. I had never been there because most of the girls thought only trash would go to there, but an old friend told me she had been and was in love with a boy from Texas whom she had met the week before. So I let her talk me into going. That was the last time I ever saw her for the boy she had the crush on was MY future husband.

There were about ten boys who had pushed their chairs up against the wall leading to the girls' bathroom so they could check us out as we came in and headed for the mirrors. And there he was. Black curls, dark brown eyes, broad shoulders and a shy smile. That was it! This was the boy in my imagination and he liked me.

He asked me to dance and then said I wasn't a very good dancer so could we just sit down and talk. Many years later I realized it was he who was the lousy dancer, but I was glad to sit down and talk. Actually, I just wanted to look at him and I loved the way he looked at me.

Six months later I was married and living in Texas. My first lesson in manifesting had come true. His name was Gary and he couldn't have been sweeter. He was incredibly romantic; showered me with presents and left love notes all over the apartment. We planned a perfect life together. He took a new job which required him to travel four days a week and I was working as a secretary. I didn't know anyone in Dallas but I made friends easily and took classes in the evenings, so his being gone didn't bother me too much. The three days he was home each week were like a honeymoon. We were totally in love.

Before the end of the first year we had a perfect son and seventeen months later, another part of my plan, a beautiful daughter. We had saved up enough money for a down payment on a perfect little house in the perfect neighborhood. My life was like a fairytale with no wicked stepmother. We rocked along in that myth for fourteen years during which time we added another perfect child, a daughter.

Then…Gary started his own business and stopped traveling. I was not ready for this much reality. Seven days a week he was home. What was that all about? This turned my world upside down. Cooking, smiling all the time, keeping the air-conditioning turned to a temperature that was pleasant for him while I wore a jacket, having to let him know when I was having PTA or other meetings at the house. This was really annoying.

But we struggled and adjusted and I got a job teaching tap dancing and he was making good money. We bought a lake house and a boat and added one more piece of perfection to this scenario, another perfect daughter. But twenty years into this story, Gary and I weren't so perfect anymore. The picture still looked great, but the glue holding the frame together was coming apart at the corners. We were cranky. He loved sporting events, I hated them. He loved to read pop fiction and tell me about the gory stories; I put my hands over my ears. He loved action-adventure movies, I waited in the lobby. He loved to scuba-dive, I am afraid of deep water. He loved to bike, I prefer to walk. He liked to smoke dope, I don't even drink wine. I like huge parties, he is reclusive. I am fascinated by UFO's and other phenomenon, he thinks that is all nuts.

The kids and I are active in our synagogue; he only goes for special events like weddings. I believe in reincarnation, he thinks this is all there is. And even though there were still a lot of things we did enjoy together, country music, gardening, James Kavanaugh, live theater, concerts in the park, comedians, long Sunday brunches in nice restaurants without the kids, and making love, my heart hurt a lot. This was not what I thought the middle of my marriage would be. I wanted to be in love. We loved each other obsessively, but not in a good way anymore. We both set out to make the other one "see the light" and adjust.

Someone had to win but that meant someone else had to lose. It sure seemed easier for him to be like me than for me to change to his liking. No one mentioned compromise.

So we quit living together for a while and we were sad. So we lived together again and we were sad. Then we only lived together on weekends and that was better. But it wasn't right, wasn't what we really wanted to do. We wanted things to be the way they were before. We forgot that we had to end that story together, that we had a sacred contract with each other to make it work.

Then he got sick with a cancer. And they cut out the cancer but he got real scared and then the depression and then the cancer came back. I can't write about those eighteen months because it is still too painful and when I see the words that tell of his pain and my fear and the kids feeling so helpless and in terror that daddy would die; it makes me cry all over again.

When my sweetheart was scared of something, he had to face it and get it over with. He was terrified of dying. So he got up one morning and violently took himself to another dimension. I don't know if he had already planned to exit or not but the last night he was here; he wrote me the most romantic love letter of all, a letter so revealing that it closed up all the wounds from our recent unhappy history. He gave me the freedom to once again be in love with that boy from the dance hall.

But that suicide is not how this story really ended. I can't let our story end like that. In my story Gary won the lottery and went for a trip around the world to study the sex life of some obscure dragonfly. And when I am very, very old...like ll2, he will come back and we will move to the farm and take long walks and he will fish from the pond and clean out fence rows while I drive into town to buy R.C. Cola and Moon Pies for him. And should I grow tired of waiting and marry someone else, that nice man will only be my lover, not my husband; I've already had a husband.

TANG

(My English Name is Sara)
April 19, 2004
Women's Retreat, Austin Texas
Vietnamese, pretty
Grew up in Viet Nam

I was thirteen of eighteen children. Just about every year and half my mother give birth. She was strong woman. She lived to be 89. My father was successful businessman. Then the war and then the war finally stop and I do not know what to do, where to go. I cannot find any of my family; some were dead, others taken away. There is no money, no home, no parents or grandparents I can find. So I run. I run until I get to boats but I do not know where boats go to. I do not care; I just get on one and to wherever it take me. Long time passes and I am in Fort Chaffee, Arkansas. Someone show me map of Dallas, Texas and a place there called Highland

Park. They tell me lady there will sponsor me, so I say, "Okay, I to Texas. I go Highland Park."

I meet nice lady and she very good to me but I no good at housework. I very bad at cleaning and so I tell her I very good at sewing and she find me job at sewing.

Many years pass and I get my own apartment with help of lady and I start sewing business. I become very, very lonesome. I think my heart breaking or may be disappearing. I do not laugh for long, long time. Then I meet David's father. He make me laugh. We are together much of the time. I do not laugh for so long time, when I say goodnight, my face hurts he make me laugh so very much. He take me to nice places, teach me to dance, hold my hand in movies.

On my birthday he give me brown puppy and gold ring he has written on it, "you are my love." I very happy. Then he tells me he has wife and daughter in Viet Nam. Already I be with him two years. I devastated. I think all blood has left my body. I make him go away but it is too late for I have been with him. I have lay with him like a wife. He go away and I have boy baby. I never tell him. He bring wife and daughter to Dallas. I never see them, it is too painful.

That twenty years ago. I never look at other man. David's father, he still have my heart. Nights, I close my eyes and he still be with me; he still make me laugh. He is my very own man in my head. Also in my heart. He always be my only man.

TESSA

September 13, 2003
Met through friends at Dallas Museum of Art
Red hair to her waist, classically beautiful

*B*efore I tell this story, let me tell you a little bit about myself. I have always been a good girl except for that one thing. I always went to church, never sassed my parents or teachers, made good grades, and was a cheerleader at my school. I've been proud of being good. My friends will tell you that I was very square growing up. I got married when I was twenty-one, just out of college and to the only boy I had ever slept with. So, please don't judge me by what I am about to share with you. I just want someone to understand what happened and why. I need to tell this and feel there are others out there who have done, or might have done, what I did. I guess I'm just tired of feeling so alone. I want someone to know why this happened and that I didn't mean to hurt anyone.

I love my husband. He did me wrong...real wrong. Right after we moved to Lubbock, right after our fifth wedding anniversary, he started to have girlfriends. He was a doctor, playing God in the daytime and being bored with me after work. I was still in school, trying to be an archeologist, but I wasn't interesting enough. We had just found out that he couldn't have children without a lot of work because he had a low sperm count. I guess he took that to mean he could sleep around and not worry about it. It was 1969 and I didn't want to divorce him. We had a life here, social events every weekend and a certain status with the medical school. And I really loved him even if he did hurt me all the time. So I stayed with him, finishing my degree and went to work at the University.

In 1979 I had an opportunity to take a group of students on a three month dig in Arizona to work with the very famous Charles Lambert. Things happened there that summer. Richard came to visit me four times, each time he was very obviously not interested in me and was anxious to get back to Lubbock. After he left the first time, Charles saw the tears in my eyes as I turned and walked back to our quarters after saying goodbye to Richard. He put his arms around me; I fell into him and that is how it began.

He was a widower with a son, twelve at the time, and old enough to be my dad, but one of those ageless men who belongs to no time or generation. We became lovers immediately and although it was the most blissful time of my life, I always knew I would never leave Richard and I don't even know if he would have wanted me to. We were just together. After we made love we would lie together for hours talking, just being happy to know each other. The summer ended and I returned to Lubbock, to Richard. Something had changed. We made love like when we were kids and I was glad — for I had known before returning to Lubbock that I was pregnant by Charles. So I just let Richard believe that all of that lovemaking had created a miracle. Our son was born on April 6, 1980 and he looked just like me. Richard was delighted and we named him Aiden, after my father.

I never heard from Charles again until that day in 1996 when he appeared at our front door. Richard and Aiden were playing with the dogs out in the backyard when the bell rang. I thought I was going to pass out when I saw Charles standing there. Terrified, I led him into the living room and called to the boys to come in and meet him. During the conversation he told us that his son had been killed in a car accident and he was leaving Arizona — going somewhere on the East Coast.

Richard and Aiden had to leave to go to a soccer game and when they were gone, Charles asked if Aiden were his son. I started to deny him and had cast my eyes to the floor when he took my face in his big hands and made me look at him. "Sweet Tessa, please. I have just lost my Perry. I'm not asking anything of you, just let me know. Does he have huge flat feet? Is he left-handed? Does he have a cowlick in the front and two in the back of his hair? Does he talk in his sleep? Does he stay up all night reading?"

I started to cry and he held me as he had that first time. Then he stepped back from me, leaned and kissed my forehead. "If there is ever anything you need of me, please find me." He moved to Maine that week. We have spoken five or six times. I understand why I loved him. He nurtures me; asks nothing of me. I look at Aiden and am grateful for the gifts of fate.

CHARLENE

December 1, 2008
On phone lines for Crisis Support
Short and stocky, pleasant

ou just never know when fate will kick you in the teeth or reach out a hand to you. I've always been taught that everything you do comes back to you but what I don't understand is why it always comes back to me and not to the pricks who are really doing such terrible things. Oh...well...guess that's one of those questions made for pondering late some night when everyone is drunk or stoned.

That year had not been very good to me. Seems a dark cloud was hovering over my head and I was having trouble digging myself out of it. I was not in a relationship, not even getting over one, and I woke up that Thursday morning in the deepest funk, wanting someone I could hug...even if that was all there was to it. I just needed a

115

hug from a man who thought I was a real woman. I looked at myself in the mirror and, as we all know, when the image looking back at you meets with your approval, it is a day to make life just happen. So...I decided to go meet the big guy who had just opened a health food store in my neighborhood. I had seen him looking at me with curiosity and so I put on my most flattering outfit and went down there.

He was delighted to be the object of my attention. We made a date. He left a romantic poem on my voice mail. We went out that night and every night for a month. He was not aggressive about initiating sex and I was loving the tenderness and so I pretended I was in no hurry either. It was one of the biggest lies of my life. He would stop by my house on his way to work and we would just lie on the couch, wrapped in each other.

Then we went away for a weekend and it was so wonderful I can't write about it, like something out of a movie just before the wife walks in. But there was no wife to walk in, no children...nothing to mess this up. But it was messed up before we got started. My dream man had terrible demons he was wrestling with, intensified by being bi-polar and not very good at taking his medication.

That was twelve years ago and I'm still with him, we're still in love. I didn't know about his illness and that wouldn't have stopped me anyway. We had a marvelous wedding in Muir Woods, the guests and attendants in Celtic attire, the High Priestess performed a hand-fasting ceremony so beautiful it brought everyone to tears. We still spend a few minutes each morning, lying on the couch, wrapped in each other. Usually I cry for I don't know what monster will come home to me after his day is through. I go to a support group for wives and husbands of bi-polar people and the group gets smaller all the time for it seems only the strongest stay...the others either divorce or commit suicide.

Every day is a new adventure and the saving grace is that sometimes we have a whole week of good days. Maybe it sounds childish to believe in soul-mates, but I do. And I believe my dear, miserable husband is my soul-mate, and he loves me as I love him. There is always that little bit of knowing that tomorrow one little bit of chemistry could go awry and everything we have could blow up in our faces. He's learned to "feel" episodes coming on now, so he can leave work and be alone, out of the way of someone he might harm. Please don't misunderstand. This is NOT a sad story. I would not give up this love we have for each other for stability without him...not for an hour.

CISSIE ANN

May 11, 2005
On phone lines for crisis support.
Small, delicate brunette
Grew up in Jackson, Mississippi.

It is a funny thing how incest works on your brain and holds you prisoner of your memories for ever and ever. My daddy didn't kiss nor make me touch him or put his penis inside me. He would wash me. He washed me until I was a grown-up woman. We were well-to-do, white socialites in a small town in Alabama. I had a coming-out and everything a proper white girl in the sixties did. No one would have believed what was going on in our family. See, Mother was a drunk. I don't know to this day if anyone outside the family knew it and my only sibling, my sister, Darla, has been drunk for forty years. When Mother would get drunk and pass out, Daddy would look at me and say, "I think you need a good

119

washing up, Sunshine." I would plead and cry and kick and scream but to no avail.

It all started when I was about two and never did anyone protect me. I finally told my health teacher when I was eleven but by then Daddy was a Judge and she just didn't want to ruin her life by helping me. I can pretty much understand that, sometimes. Anyway, he would take me up to the big bathroom upstairs where there would be a bubble bath already drawn for me. The tub was elevated up on a two-foot platform, and so he didn't even have to stoop over to wash me.

First, he would direct me as to how he wanted me to take my clothes off, which garment first. He would take the washcloth and wash my face and neck and armpits and then gently, gently, my nipples even before there was even any sign of me developing. Lastly, he would slide his hand underneath my bottom, lingering on the labia. I would close my eyes and try to think of anything else, but his seductive voice would bring me back. He would say, over and over, "only your daddy knows how to wash you, little darling. Only daddy loves you enough to get you real clean." When he was finished, he would dry me off, put my pajamas on me and send me off with, "This is just our secret, Sweetheart, because daddy loves you the best."

When Mother got real bad off with her drinking, we hired a big black woman named Marlene to keep the house. She was a wise woman and didn't take any bossing from anyone. The first time daddy fixed a bath for me; she got right in his face and said, "That child is way too old for you to bathe, Judge Sloan. I think she can rightly take care of herself." He never touched me again. But, by then, the damage had been done.

My attempts at relationship and marriage were total disasters. I would go from hating sex to not being able to get enough of it, going from one therapist to another. Then a miracle happened. One day in group I heard of a therapist who was a recovered incest victim and I made an appointment with her the coldest day of 1999 and, desperate and freezing, I kept the appointment.

When I sat down across the desk from her, she looked right into my soul and said to me, "Guess you're tired of thinking about daddy every time you want to get off, huh?" Crude, confrontational, direct to the gut...I liked her. She never let me whine nor feel sorry for myself and let me know in no uncertain terms that his behavior was not about me. If it had not been me he abused, it would have been someone else, and that was the beginning of my healing. My husband goes to all the sessions with me and, for him, I will have a healing. Well, mostly for me.

AUBREY

September 11, 2006
Chicago, Illinois
Women's Retreat
Cute, big smile
Grew up in Valparaiso, Indiana

Valparaiso isn't quite as cold as Chicago, but it is almost. And the January my husband left was the coldest in 56 years. He totally blindsided me with his announcement.

My parents had died when I was nine, in a train wreck, and I had been raised by an old auntie who was more like a cranky, crusty old man. She smoked cigars, spit on the sidewalk, wore sensible shoes and had never married. All of my growing up there was a parade of men "visiting". To call her plain-spoken would be an understatement. The visitors could not be identified by type for they were every type and they always left in a better mood than when they came in. The word prostitution never entered my mind. But this story begins when Shithead moved out.to find himself.

We had three awesome daughters, ages seven, eight and nine. I insisted that he tell the girls he was leaving, and why. "I've been offered a job with an oil company in Yemen, girls, and I can't afford to turn it down. It will make us very rich in a few years. I promise to call every week." His real name is Peter and I'm certain his mother must have known she was naming him after a sex organ. He could lie without blinking and the girls believed every word of it.

When he left he gave me a check for $5,000 and a big smile as if he were giving me a million dollars. "This should take care of you all for a while." I had no job skills, no resources at all, and our rent was $800.00 a month. Valparaiso isn't a place for single, unemployable moms to live and prosper.

Aunt Lucille met me for breakfast after I dropped the kids off at school. How do you tell a woman you love that she needs to shave? She greeted me with a big hug and an abundance of enthusiasm. "We'll work it out; Hon. This is not the end of the world."

Throughout breakfast she let me cry and call him names and feel sorry for myself and the girls, listening carefully as she had always done as my mom. "Listen, Aubrey. I've been giving this a lot of thought and I know how you could make a good living and still stay at home for the kids. A lot of people are making money with 800 numbers these days."

"You mean with psychic hot lines?"

"No, honey, I mean with sex hot lines."

I almost fell out of the booth. "God, Mom you've got to be kidding. I don't know anything about sex. That's probably why Peter left us".

"Peter left you because he is a selfish, self-centered asshole. You don't need to know anything about sex. I have lots of books for you. How do you think I supported us and bought all of those rent houses? I was a prostitute, sweetie. Those visitors were there for sex. You're looking a little sick...it's okay".

"But Mom... you went to church every Sunday."

"So what... God loves prostitutes. We serve a great need."

"I could never do sex with strangers. Nothing bad about you, but I just couldn't do it."

"It's a different world now honey. You don't have to do it, you just have to talk about it and you have a real sexy voice".

Two hours later we were in a book store in Calumet City, Indiana, buying books on sex. Over the next month, Lucille taught me how to detach from everything I read or heard on the phone, to just become sort of a sexual zombie with a voice, responding to a lot of lonely men. Six weeks after Peter left, I was connected six hours a day to a sex hot line, paying me $25.00 per hour. The company installed a private phone line for business and Lucille got me a portable hands-free set so that I could do my housework while I answered the phones.

After a while it wasn't so bad for she was right, I really could detach. I was making $150.00 per day, five days a week and always available for the girls. I told them I was stuffing envelopes and doing other odd jobs. This was 1989. In 1993, just before my thirty-fifth birthday, Mama Lucille died from her cigars and vodka and six months later I was diagnosed with breast cancer.

The girls and I had no one. They had never heard from Peter after the conversation about going to Yemen. His folks did not respond to their letters. As they grew older, I had covered my career choice to them by telling them I was doing telemarketing for a non-profit agency.

Scout, who was now thirteen, became the house mother. She took over delegating all of the household chores to Sophie and Brittany. My neighbors took turns driving me for the chemo treatments after the first surgery to remove the left breast. Acting totally against the rules, over the years I had developed a friendship with one of the regular callers, a nursing student who lived just minutes away in Lansing. He seemed a safe confidant.

We never exchanged our real names but I knew he was 29 and about to graduate. He called every day after my first surgery, just to check up on me. The sex calls stopped; he became an anonymous friend, willing to pay for the privilege of calling. He begged to meet me. I would not for it would have cost me my job, which I continued to do as soon as I felt better. I never told him my real name or the names of my daughters. He didn't even know I lived in Valparaiso.

When the first check-up showed that I needed additional surgery, the other breast and the lymph nodes, I fell apart on the phone to him. I told him my real first name was Aubrey and he said his was Jason. He actually cried with me. On a Monday, two weeks after that conversation, sometime mid-morning, there was a knock at my door, a persistent knocker who wouldn't go away.

I dragged my haggard body to the door, opened it, and standing there was a tall, blonde young man with the bluest eyes I had ever seen. He was holding flowers! "Aubrey, it's Jason. May I come in?" The next hour was a fog for me. I had to go back to bed and he sat on the side of my bed and told me how he had found me. He was not a nursing student, but an intern in oncology at the hospital where I had my surgery. It was a miracle that we had never met.

I let him hold me. Let him see the scars. He even made me laugh. He didn't seem like a stranger at all, but an old friend. I got well. We dated for a year but we weren't really dating for we already knew each other intimately. I got over the difference in our ages and my scars, things that had never bothered him. I even told him about my precious Mama Lucille.

So it's been six years since the first diagnosis. Jason and I have been married two years and it just gets better every year. Against Jason's wishes I may have implants soon. He doesn't want me to traumatize my body any more, .but I might. Oh...and by the way...he was shocked to find out that I learned all that sex stuff from books and so he is helping me with my clinicals! It's a good life.

TAMAR

September 24, 2006
Women's Retreat Chicago, Illinois
Brown skin, green eyes, average frame, pretty
Grew up in Hammond, Indiana

He died last month and it was the saddest funeral I have ever attended. Not just because he was only 49, but because he was so loved by so many people. "Mikey" was his nickname because of the old T.V. commercial about Mikey eating everything. Our Mikey, at his lightest weight was probably still way over 350 pounds. He was tall, but not tall enough to carry a body that sometimes climbed up to 450 pounds or more. Sure, he died of heart disease brought on by that enormous girth and the fats he consumed daily.

I moved to San Diego to get away from the cold and a family of religious fanatics back in Chicago. It took two years of living in a rented room eating peanut butter to save enough for the trip and one month's rent when I got here. Two months after I arrived, I met Mikey. This was in 1983 and he owned one of the first metaphysical bookstores in the city. It might have been the only one back then. I was excited to be in this magical, beautiful California but having a hard time making friends and incredibly lonely.

Mikey spotted me the moment I walked into the bookstore. We talked…he made me smile…then he made me laugh and pretty soon I was in love. I didn't care that he was this huge fat man, married, and somewhat of a smart-ass and tease. He was not just a ray of sunshine in my life, he was the sun, and I wanted all I could get of him.

After three months of daily visits to the bookstore he took me home to meet his wife and kids…said he wanted me to see what I was getting into before we started anything. My own skin is dark brown but he was so black he made me look white by comparison and his wife, Mia, looked like some Swedish beauty queen. She was very nice to me, so nice, in fact that I felt there must be some sort of understanding between them regarding women in his life. I knew I wasn't the first…and there were others who followed me.

We became lovers. He was clear with me that this was just a transition period for me and that he could only give me one year of his life. He pretended nothing…was very clear that he loved Mia but enjoyed other women in many different roles. (I'm over forty now and I have been with more than one man…with men of colors and ethnicity.) I want to tell you my biggest surprise about Mikey. This man, Mikey, had the smallest penis I have yet to see. Erect, it couldn't have been over an inch and a half long. Plus I had to find it under all that belly. Then it became almost like a game to decide what I would do with it once I had my fingers on it.

With that in mind, I tell you Mikey was the greatest lover I have ever experienced. He just had this loving, sensual, tender, whispery, teasing, and playful, oral, digital, way of making me squeal with joy. I was obsessed with our love. I knew he loved me. I couldn't have imagined the kindness that came out of him towards me. He couldn't possibly have faked any of our times together. He watched me grow into my new life; guided me in my work, friendships, and helped me select books to learn from. It seemed every week he introduced me to someone new who enriched me.

Then my year was up. The last six weeks, he pushed me out of his life and then set me free. I had moments so dark I thought I would never see the light again. It took more than two years to get over him but I did finally make a good life for myself here...an excellent life. His funeral was filled with women whom I suspect had experienced Mikey just as I had. I don't feel jealous...I feel blessed to have been a part of his life...even for such a little while. There will never be a day I don't miss him.

This may sound selfish but I hope in death he will choose me and be my guardian angel.

CAROLINE

August 1, 2009
Women's Retreat, Austin, Texas.
Gray hair to waist, clear skin, handsome
Grew up in Ft. Worth, Texas

I thought he was a pretty normal guy. He had a responsible job, had been married and had grown kids. Well, he didn't speak to them...had a decent relationship with his mom. We dated for a year secretly because we both worked for the same Ad agency where there was a policy against inner-company dating. Finally, not wanting to keep it a secret anymore, I quit the job and took a sales position. When I moved into his house I thought it was the beginning of our riding off into the sunset together. I really loved this man.

He was serious and smart and knew everything about so many subjects and among many other things; we had a love of old movies in common. Although he was

133

only a few years my senior, he always acted as if he were the wiser and I would go along with it because I thought he needed me to...and besides...it didn't hurt me to pretend. Almost immediately after I moved in with him he started throwing out any of my clothes that he didn't like. I would come home from work and find spaces in my closet.

He said he was just getting rid of things that didn't flatter me. I trusted him for he was a photographer and he had an eye for things I didn't understand. Then he replaced my tooth-brush with one he thought would be better for my teeth. He bought all new make-up for me, insisted I become a blonde and talked me into buying a different car. A year later I woke up and realized there was no part of me that I recognized. I got scared.

Little things started to happen. I had brought home some poems that one of the guys at work wrote for his girlfriend. When Lester saw them he took them into the bathroom and used them for toilet paper. He insisted I return them to my friend in that condition and of course I didn't, but I did put them into my car. One day the neighbor parked his car with about a foot of it extended into our driveway. The next day his tires were slashed and from then on instances like that began to occur frequently.

I panicked and moved out while he was away. He came to my work, begging me to come back; said he had been going through a bad time and that he would be good from then on...that all he needed was my love to ground him. So I went back. He became adorable. I had never been so happy. Everything we did turn out well and I would wake up nights, thanking God for this man. I didn't understand why he had done those horrible things in the beginning but I was certain nothing like that would ever happen again. Until those dogs died...

One of our neighbors had two of those yappy little dogs. You know, the kind that bark for no reason. Well, the neighbor left the dogs outside in the daytime and Lester often worked at home the first two hours of the day, setting up client calls and planning his day. If the wind changed, those dogs would bark. Now, most people would learn to ignore them but not Lester. They really became his obsession. It was a Tuesday night that I found the hot dogs in the refrigerator. Lester was very careful with his diet, only eating the most expensive cuts of beef and he often talked about white trash who ate hot dogs. I asked him what they were for. He laughed and said he was going to photograph them. When the vet came back to the neighbor with the autopsy, it revealed the dogs had been poisoned with hot dogs soaked in anti-freeze.

I'm living in Seattle now. He is, I hope, still in Arizona. Thank God I didn't marry him and he never had a need to know my Social Security Number. Even though I know enough now to fully realize that he is crazy enough to kill me, I still miss him. I still remember the good times with him and sometimes find myself longing for him. Oh, not the guy who killed the dogs, but the one who loved me so well and made me laugh. I know that sounds sick and I am in a group, working through it, but sometimes your brain doesn't always want to go into DELETE as quickly as you would like or need.

PHOEBE

May 8, 2010
Car repair waiting room
Greenville, Texas
Short, slender, athletic, Greek, beautiful
Grew up in Houston, Texas

I went to his funeral today. I was shaking like a leaf. My grown children thought I had to go to finally close that chapter of my life. Our town is so small that everyone was there and their heads almost snapped off as they turned to look at me coming through that door.

I married him when I was sixteen and he was seventeen. He promised me the world. My old-world parents had their marriage arranged for them by their parents and they hated each other every day of my life, but stayed together and no one knew...except me of course. Lance Everett was popular at school and when he asked me for that first date, I couldn't believe it; couldn't

137

believe he had even noticed me. I was tall and dark, with coarse straight hair and black eyes. He was like a blonde, blue-eyed god and his ancestors had been Americans for ten generations...and, his folks liked me. In fact, right after we started dating, his mom said to me, "I hope you stick with him, he don't have them fits like he used to." I was too timid to ask what she meant.

Anyway, we married in 1972 and I stayed with him for twenty-five years. He beat me most every day after the first year. I couldn't tell my parents because I didn't want to worry them and, anyway, they believed you had to lie in the bed you made. I knew very well what they would say to me. So we didn't go around them or his folks either. We moved out here in the middle of nowhere and started this business I'm in now. I had three babies and he never hit me when I was pregnant. If I would say, "How come you never hit me when I was carrying your child," he would hit me harder the next time. Once he knocked out six teeth with one blow. I just bought a lot of makeup and wore dark glasses to work.

I didn't believe I had the option of leaving him. I wonder sometime if I would have left him if he had used alcohol or drugs... which he didn't...he was just mean. People, therapists, and teachers always ask me what happened to turn my life around and I truly don't know.

One morning I got up a very different person than the one who had gone to sleep the night before. I went to the bank and took half of our savings and moved it into an account in my name. I went to a lawyer and asked for

138

papers to make the business legally half mine, no matter what. I stopped at the grocery store and picked up two dozen boxes and, when I got home, I packed up everything in this house that rightfully belonged to him, emptied the garage, everything. Later, I put everything very neatly out on the lawn by the road and, all by myself, changed the locks on the doors and made sure all the window locks worked. It was like somebody else took over my body. When I had finished all of this I went to the junior college down the road and enrolled in a program to finish high school. (I am now finishing an undergraduate degree in psychology and have plans for many more. My new passion is education.)

Lance came home that day and I was hiding inside the house with a loaded shotgun, just in case, but he didn't even look towards the house. He picked up the note I had written, started throwing the boxes into the back of his pickup and drove off. We never spoke again. Not a word. At the weddings of our children, our eyes never met. As far as I know, he never dated and neither have I. I don't know what his excuse was, but I was too scared to, scared he would hurt somebody. When I walked up to that casket today, I halfway expected him to jump up and hit me. But he's dead, whoever he was, he's dead. The boy I married died twenty-nine years ago.

By the way...the note I left on his boxes of stuff...all it said was, "Don't ever come inside this house again."

BETTE EPSTEIN

TRACI

August 22, 2010
Grief Workshop Dallas, Texas
Tiny, dark hair and huge eyes
Grew up in Dallas

I was born into a comfortable family in 1972. By comfortable, I mean we took trips to foreign countries, I had my own designer, decorated bedroom, got a new car when I turned sixteen and had a clothing allowance. But I wasn't a total slug. Dad made each of us get a job as soon as we were big enough to do something. We were community people and a very tight family. I loved my life.

Our house was always filled with many and interesting people, teenagers, cats, dogs, birds, fish, and strangers who needed a place to stay for a while. Someone once said our house was like something from a J.D. Salinger novel. Mother was a talent agent when Dallas

141

was the third coast in film making. Every holiday there was a big gathering of musicians, actors, theater people and lots of stories and laughter.

There were five of us kids and not one of us ever understood the word SHY. I grew up on PAC MAN, and Rocky Horror, and boys with big hair. I didn't have much talent in any one thing and just enough in a lot of things to stay confused about a career choice so my undergraduate degree took seven years. It didn't matter. I was learning life's lessons in the meantime and my parents were very patient with me.

When I was in the second year of this degree I met Elon. He was attending one of the many colleges I went to, on a Masters MBA program, totally funded by his folks, so he had plenty of time for me. We often talked about how lucky we were to have been born into the families we had; families with so much love and seemingly well-adjusted and affluent.

He was truly the sweetest boy I had ever met. He couldn't do enough for me. The first time he slept over, he brought breakfast to bed but not until he had gone for fresh bagels, the newspaper, and one red rose. He just had it all. His manners were impeccable, his voice and demeanor delightful. When he held my hand, it was gentle and reassuring. My folks were crazy about him and comforted to see me actually liking a guy for any length of time.

After dating for two years my parents gave us the most glorious wedding in our backyard. Strolling violins, fans hung from the trees, lily-pads in the pool, and after the sun went down the entire yard was lit up with twinkling lights, even my old swing set. We were so in love.

Life was like some magical dream for over a year and then Elon began to complain about being tired all the time. We ignored it, tried to eat better and exercise more but by the end of the second year he was obviously stricken with something. He had so many tests for such a long time, one diagnosis after another. Finally, all the doctors agreed, it was leukemia. Have you ever been blindsided? It's like someone hits you in the head with a baseball bat and sends you reeling for what feels like eternity. We had so many second opinions, more tests, considered alternative treatments, got on a list for bone-marrow donors, and cried.

Six more months passed and I came home from school one day and he was gone. Gone. All of his fishing rods, bicycle, and fishing clothes—gone. Then I found the note. "Don't marry anyone else. I will be back. I have to be alone and think about this." The strangest thing; I didn't panic. I didn't even call his folks or mine for almost a week. I saw the therapist every day, but wanted to do this without the support of my family, for now. This was just my way of doing it.

Then there was the telephone call— a message left on the machine at a time when he knew I would be in school. "I need more time, maybe a month — I love you." Then I told the family. I have yet to see so many people have the exact same reaction to anything. Everyone, parents, siblings, nieces, and nephews — they all said he was doing what he had to do and we should not panic. Just wait. So we did. At the end of that month, he came home. Said he had been camping out just outside Durango, making peace with the fact that he might not live to see thirty.

We had a year of terrible treatments, a year of hope, another year of sadness and then his life ended.

Yes, I am still young, and yes, I may love again. But how will I know when it is time? When will I ever believe he isn't coming back? How could he be here today, and then — whoof — he's gone? When will I stop talking to him, writing him love letters, watching old movies of him when he was a child, of our wedding, of when we were— well, when we were — us?

EMILY

March 19, 1999
Grief workshop
Glendale, California

*T*oday I will uncover the mirrors. For all I care about looking at myself, I could have left them covered. The love of my life is resting in peace and I am trying to figure out how to join him without making a mess.

Being carved from Adam's rib did not make Eve any more a part of Adam than Seth was a part of me, and I of him. He waited forty-four years for me. I was sixty-five when we married and we never mentioned the years we waited, nor did he ever speak in any way despairingly of my husband. It was the times we grew up in, the place.

145

We were from small towns in the Midwest and met in Chicago when I was a student at the Teacher's College and he was establishing himself in his career. It was a cold day in June of 1939. I was waiting for a trolley on Michigan Avenue, coat and scarf pulled tight against my chin when he came out of the office building. Our eyes met. He stopped for a split second and then went on.

This scene repeated itself for weeks before he spoke. By the first of August we were meeting regularly for coffee and sweets every morning. Then there were dinner dates and films. We fell in love. We made love for the first time the Sunday evening after Thanksgiving when each of us had returned from visiting our families. We were both virgins but there was no fumbling, no tears. I WAS his rib... and he knew how to love me from that very first time.

I had spoken to my parents of him when I was with them and they were adamant. "Not of that religion, you don't." And my religion had not met with any more favor with his family either. The irony of this whole religion thing is that neither of us really cared about religion. By the time we were old enough to know what we were, we realized we were both secular humanists.

We never officially lived together in Chicago but we became inseparable, always careful not to leave personal items in the other's apartment because both sets of parents had a way of paying surprise visits. Because I had rushed back from the holidays to be with Seth for New Years of 1939, my parents contacted his and there was this conference with the six of us and it was decided for the best interests of both families and any potential grandchildren, we would stop seeing each other. My mother never left my side after that meeting, so there was no chance for us to be together again alone.

I had no money, no job; I was totally dependent on my parents and I was sent to San Francisco to live with an old aunt. In 1940, long distance telephone calls were outrageously expensive and the only way to communicate was through letters. I know it is a corny old story, but Aunt Thelma intercepted mine from Seth and I thought he had abandoned me. When she died, Aunt Thelma left everything to me. It was then, going through her things, that I found the mail. But it was far too late for I had married and had children by the time that happened. I won't write about my love for Joseph. He was a good man and gave me five grand and glorious children.

Once I had Seth's letters, I found him once again, still in Chicago. Each year from then on, when I visited my parents, there was a visit to Seth first. Seth never married. Both Joseph and Seth became very wealthy but Seth never came west to visit me. He said he couldn't bear it.

As the money grew and the children became adults and moved away, my visits to Chicago became more frequent. My parents were old and needed to see me. I never spoke with friends or relatives about Seth, but my brother knew. He never held it against me. When Joseph died in 1982, it was my dear brother who contacted Seth.

The day after the first anniversary of Joseph's death, Seth and I married. And we never spent another night apart...until now. We lived each other. I know my children resented him at first and my grandchildren felt abandoned by me, but it didn't matter. Only Seth mattered. Only US!

We saw the world together; the whole world and we made love in every great city with as much passion as that December 31, 1939 in Chicago. His body never failed to respond to me, even near the end. It was as if we had so much making up to do...for all the years we were separated.

Although my children never knew of my meetings with Seth in Chicago, only Chloe became close with him. I'm not angry about that. They loved their father, loved our lives we had together and I knew it was hard on them having this strange man move into their father's house so soon and seeing a glow in me they had never seen before. They all came together for me these final weeks. They were all there for me as he lay dying and he had a peaceful passing at home. I don't feel sorry for myself...we had almost twenty years of a being together that was so true, so complete that it must have already spanned many lifetimes together. When the crying has stopped, I'll be fine. He's waiting for me...again.

ROSIE

Glendale, California
Hypnosis conference
Too much sun, too much skin
Topeka, Kansas

I met Sandy fifteen years ago in a hypnosis training class in Santa Fe. Sandy is a nickname because of his hair color. He is actually Cuban but no one believes him since he is tall, has very high hips and light eyes. But boy, when he dances, there is no doubt. I guess that is when I first fell in love with him.

We've never made love. Fifteen years of not being able to touch one another except on the dance floor and I'm not so sure how much longer I can do this. In the beginning it was so much fun, having a crush on someone who was as unavailable as I was. I felt like I was in elementary school. He loved me immediately also. His story was this. He had been married at that time for

149

fifteen years. We were both 45 and very devoted to our spouses.

It started the first day of the two week seminar. We were learning to do the standing induction and when I fell into his arms and he held me to his chest, I felt as if I would faint. Everyone thought he had done such a good job with the induction that I couldn't come out of the hypnosis, but it was a different kind of hypnosis.

I am Mexican, Catholic, and very committed to my marriage and my husband. We don't have any children because of bad things that happened to me when I was a child, and I cannot conceive. Oscar, my husband, did not want to have a child without me, so we never adopted nor hired a surrogate. And we loved each other deeply since we were sixteen. We have a great life and I will never hurt him by revealing my feelings for Sandy. And Sandy is in a happy, committed marriage of many years and one child.

Now the reader may be thinking that I am kidding myself about this great love I have for Oscar if I can be totally in love with Sandy, but there are lots of different kinds of love and one should try not to judge. Oscar and I grew up together; we lived next door to one another, actually. Sandy and his wife met in college where each of them was doing graduate work in psychology. She is a beautiful blonde Anglo.

Shortly after falling in love with Sandy, I did a complete makeover on myself. I got new breasts, way too large for my small frame. I changed my hair color to blonde and had some work done on my face. In some crazy way, I thought I could compete with her if I looked like her. The first time we met after the change, Sandy was very sad that I had done this. I gave up the blonde hair but it was too late to fix the boobs for I couldn't afford it at that time. Now I like the attention they create when I walk into a room. I will probably have them removed one day.

The Santa Fe school was just the beginning. Sandy and I began going to every class all over the country if we could find the time and money to be away for these trips are very costly. We have often shared a room, separate beds and we truly never sleep together. We both know we could not do that without making love. We have not shared a passionate kiss. Sometimes I wonder if this experience is laying the groundwork for my ending this lifetime as a nun.

Our physical contact all happens on the dance floor. We never go to a conference that doesn't have a banquet and dance. We go onto the dance floor the minute the music starts and stay there usually until midnight.

We live in separate cities but we stay in contact almost daily by email and phone calls (which we send and receive during our workdays). Fifteen years! Sometimes I wonder how this happened. I look at the age in me now and am saddened that soon I will not be attractive naked should we ever be able to make love. I guess that is shallow.

Do I feel we have cheated our spouses? No, not at all. In fact, the inspiration I have from my love for Sandy and his love for me creates in me a desire to be an excellent wife. I don't believe you can love too many people. It is just unfortunate that in our world, love has to be pure and simple and exclude anyone with whom your connection is not socially acceptable the way we conduct ourselves. He didn't say he wants to end it, but he is saying a lot about how much he loves me...would never want to hurt me... and that he feels we were just star-crossed lovers. I see that expression a lot and still don't really know what it means. I guess the stars were just not going the same way for both of us.

I don't know what a soul-mate is and don't know if I believe in that. I do believe we were destined to share what we shared. Would we have been happy in a marriage together? Maybe. I will

die thinking so. If he stops seeing me soon, I will not weep for what was not, but celebrate what was. We WERE... in our own way... a beautiful destiny.

MERCEDES

July 2009
New Orleans, Louisiana
Bereavement workshop
Beautiful Jamaican woman
Grew up in Florida

J was working in a mental health clinic in Miami when Neil brought his two sons in for counseling. He was a physician and could have afforded the best care money could buy but he wanted the anonymity of this free clinic. I like to think I was the best care, and I loved this job in a part of town that was a heavy concentration of poor people of all races and ethnicities.

When we met I probably outweighed him by 150 pounds for I was easily 300 and not very tall. I looked a bit like a ball. But I sure was cute. And, he was ten years younger than me. Not a customary setting for a budding romance, right?

153

Neil's marriage had fallen apart because his wife became addicted to pain medication years prior to this because of a dental procedure. She kept this a secret from him for a long time and once he discovered it, the conflict began. She stole his script pads forged his name and when he busted her for that, she managed in many other ways to get her addiction taken care of. The kids were small and there was a nanny, so no one was the wiser for it until she ran out once on a vacation in Paris and went into a rage.

A long heartbreaking struggle to come to grips with the fact that she loved the meds more than the marriage and children. The divorce became the only way out.

His kids were great fun. They had his sense of humor and were incredibly intelligent and sophisticated for their young ages of 6 and 7. We played a lot of word games together and had outings on the beach and pretty soon Neil and I and the children were companions on most holidays and weekends. He didn't have biological family in Miami and I was an only child who never married...so it was a perfect setup for friendship. Of course I wasn't supposed to "date" the patients, but somehow this seemed to be something not like dating, but...oh, more of becoming friends.

I never allowed myself to think of him as a lover or to even daydream of him. I had been fat for so long I learned to protect myself from the heartbreak of making the first move with a regular size guy. But I was certainly no virgin for, although it may surprise the reader, there are a lot of guys of every size who love fat girls...and girls who love fat boys. I had not been deprived of a love life.

We continued this platonic routine for the entire summer break. The kids had learned to love my body and would sit in my lap or snuggle up close to me when there was any excuse. I would read to them and usually with one under each arm, cozy on the sofa. It was a good thing.

Time passed. Mark and Michael were back in school. First one week passed with no call from Neil. Then the second. Then...At the end of the third week, Neil called on Friday and asked if I would like to do something with him without the boys for they were with their mom. Of course I would. So we went to see a play and for dinner. It was easy and comfortable for both of us.

The next weekend, it was me with Neil and the boys back to our regular projects. They helped me decorate my house for Halloween and I taught them about The Day of the Dead. They loved the whole idea of celebrating the deceased ancestors and we made plans to go to the big celebration down in the Mexican community on Sunday.

On Saturday Neil called to say the kids were going to visit their grandparents, so he supposed I didn't want to take him to the celebration. Of course I did. We went. We danced in the streets with everyone else. We ate foods that neither of us could identify. And later...back at my house...we took a nap...on my very wide sofa.

It was joyous, cuddled up with him. When he woke up, he kissed the top of my head and caressed my hair. He is very tall and so he had to scooch down until his feet hung off the sofa so that we were face to face. "You are so very beautiful." Yes, he said that to me. I didn't expect it but I certainly didn't disagree. It freed me up to be comfortably romantic with him. We kissed as lovers and soon we were making love with such ease that it seemed we had done it many times before. When we were finished, I tried to sit up but he pulled me down next to him and very softly whispered into my ear... "Will you marry me?" That was the first time I thought I had imagined the whole thing. But I had not.

Fast forward...We had a sweet wedding on the beach near the Merry Go Round, where we had gone so many times with the boys. We each had five guests, the children, and the strangers passing by. I don't think anyone can describe bliss. We were so in love it must have looked sickening to anyone who spent time with us. Pretty soon we had a new house, lots of friends who enriched our lives, custody of Mark and Michael most of the time and three stray dogs who just wandered into our yard one day.

Then the tragedy...Neil had never one time mentioned my weight. He couldn't quite make his arms stretch all the way around me for a hug but we only laughed about that. Two years into this blissful life, I decided to get a gastric bypass procedure. Neil argued with me about this, but I was determined to make myself small enough for a real hug. So I did it. It was incredibly successful. Within six months I had lost 125 pounds and a year later, I was down to 124. The kids were disappointed because they missed my fat to cuddle up to, but they had reached an age where cuddling with "mom" wasn't very important anyway. Neil never praised me in any way that would make me think he had hated my fat, but at 5' tall, my new weight sure felt better, my health was excellent. And when we made love, it was so nice to hold his flat belly next to mine.

One year of this. Thank you Creator and all the powers that be! Neil had suffered severe headaches in just one spot in his head for all of his adult years. Being a physician, of course, he had himself checked out in every direction. Nothing. No family history of migraines or cluster headaches, no stress headaches, no tumors. However, he had been adopted by his stepfather after his dad died at the age of 29 of a brain "blister" they called it in the remote area where he grew up. He was always told his dad had a stroke. It was an aneurysm.

No one could know that Neil was predisposed for an aneurysm. On January 16, 2009, after a wonderful evening of a nice dinner, a coffee out on the patio, and a tender lovemaking session, Neil got up to go to the bathroom and dropped to the floor. He died on the way to the hospital.

Oh, no, don't weep for me. I've had a life. I've been loved for all the right reasons. I've loved because I wanted to. I've lost. I've gained two sons. With all of this I will now be a better counselor than I ever could have been before. I can help.

BETTE EPSTEIN

PRISCILLA

Salsa dance class
Dark hair, very fair skin
Dallas

"He's a telephone repair man, for crying out loud! Mother said.

Being born into a family with money and a certain social status has always proven to be a total pain for me. I grew up in Highland Park, went to HP schools, but that was the only place in my life where I was with normal, middle class people.

I went away to a small college in Ohio. Hated the cold, came home after the first year and Dad, who truly believed that idle hands were the devil's workshop, gave me a job in his company, just to keep me from doing something stupid, like drugs. I liked working for him. He owned an accounting firm and I quickly discovered I had a knack for every project he assigned to me. He wanted me

159

to go to school and "make something of myself" once he discovered I was smart and very task and goal oriented. Nope, I had found myself very early.

He paid me well, I bought a nice little house in Richardson, and although Mother thought it was crazy for a twenty one year old to be living alone, doing all of my own housework (seriously, how much could there be?) Dad supported me in everything I decided to do. By twenty-five, I had created a blissful little world for myself with my cat, dogs, circle of yuppie friends, hobbies, and four days a month I volunteered at one of the busiest soup kitchens. I even had a boyfriend named Chad who fit the profile of a "good catch". Yes, that expression is still used in certain circles, especially by our mothers.

A year ago I decided to do some remodeling on my house and one of the things I did was to have the telephone system updated with internet service, and a security system. So I called AT&T for a service man to come to counsel me about what I needed. He was nice, very open to my needs and when I asked him if he would like a cup of coffee, we sat down at the table for a conversation. He was so easy to talk to, very understanding and helpful. We also laughed a lot for he had a great sense of humor and a cleverly sarcastic wit.

He made a plan for me and came back the next week to supervise the installation of the changes. After the job was complete he stayed a few minutes and again we enjoyed each other. I discovered that he had a dog that he was interested in training and since I had plans to take my latest pound pup to training the next week, I asked him if he would like to bring his dog and join us.

The training session turned out to be excellent and when we said goodbye, we agreed he would also return the following week. That night I found myself excited and happy about my new friend.

Chad and I continued to see each other most weekends although we did not have a lot of the same interests we found things to do, mostly work related seminars or dinners with mutual friends. I thought I was in love with him and had been for almost a year. Our parents thought we were the perfect couple, both tall with dark hair. He had gone to the same high school, grown up in the same neighborhood, and attended the same church. How much easier could a marriage be than to someone who was so much the same? But we weren't the same, not really.

It wasn't a month before I began spending more time with Michael than I was with Chad. We discovered rock climbing together and after he taught me to country and western dance, we were at Red River dance hall at least twice each week. Chad didn't seem to mind at first but after a couple of months, he demanded an explanation. I didn't really know what to tell him. I had not given a label to my friendship with Michael. Nor had I mentioned to him that Michael is a black man, although barely dark enough to call himself one. He knew I had a steady guy, so he stayed respectful of that and never even flirted with me.

I thought I should stay with Chad because he was the perfect marriage material, and so I told him that if he needed me to, I would stop spending time with Michael. The next weekend was Valentine's Day and that evening he brought a ring and when we returned from a romantic dinner out, he proposed. I accepted and we went back to our same old structured life. But I didn't question that. I just accepted that I was supposed to do what was right. I loved my parents and never wanted to do anything to hurt or embarrass them and I knew Mother was excited about the engagement to Chad.

When I told Michael about the engagement, he sounded very sad on the telephone, but he managed to make a joke, said he would "see you round" and I didn't speak to him again for over four months. I thought about him all the time. I began staying home a lot, just reading or being miserable. Mother was pressuring me to pick a wedding date and start making plans, but I couldn't get out of bed on weekends and do anything. Chad's mom and dad invited me to go on a family trip with them and I did. I tried to be the good girlfriend and create solid friendships with my future family, but my heart was just sad.

Not sophisticated enough to recognize the difference in sad and depressed, I went to a psychotherapist for help. I talked, she smiled and nodded. Then I returned two weeks later. I talked, she smiled and nodded. Finally I asked her how long she thought it would take before I felt better. "Well, I guess that's up to you." Feeling very frustrated, I turned to the internet for help.

Pretty much everything I found led me to believe I wasn't depressed, but extremely sad. And my sadness always produced an image of Michael and a deep longing.

I knew it was a long shot, but I thought maybe since Mother had at least at one time been in love with Dad, I asked her to meet me for lunch. We had barely ordered when I just blurted it out. "Mother, I'm not in love with Chad. I'm going to end the engagement."

She just stared at me for a full minute. Then she gave me the talk about what a great catch he is, how everyone is envious of us, what a beautiful couple we are, what amazing children we will produce. I put my head down on the table and began to sob. I put my hands over my ears as she began to talk again. "You are just a little jittery now, Prissy. Every bride feels the same way. You will be just fine." I couldn't shut out her voice.

Finally I raised my voice and said to her," I don't want things to be just fine. I want to be with another man". I startled myself. She finally went silent.

Then I told her about Michael, but not about the black part. It was now her turn to be hysterical. "Priscilla. For God's sake! Are you out of your mind? He's a telephone repair man! You will not end this engagement to a perfectly wonderful man for a fling with a telephone repair man!" I stood up and walked away without saying anything more.

The sadness did not go away and I didn't break up with Chad. But I did telephone Michael. He wouldn't see me. He did, however, email me with a message about love and longing and a poem he had written after our first meeting.

> *I watched her mouth as she spoke,*
>
> *Considering the taste of coffee kisses*
>
> *And knowing the mystery would remain.*
>
> *Girl already promised you hold my heart.*

So what could I do? Devastated, I phoned Dad. He came to my house and held me while I sobbed. Then he told me of the scrappy little country girl he had met when, at sixteen, he had gone on a fishing trip with his uncle. He talked about love and longing and making the right choice. "I never loved your mother like I loved Lilly, but I had so many others to consider." He said that except for having me, he had so many times wished he had not considered anything except his own heart.

"Do this...close your eyes and imagine spending the rest of your life without one of them, then the other. You will make the right choice."

"Dad...I didn't tell you this...he's black."

Dad was quiet for about ten seconds and then he said, "Well, then. I would guess the first thing you have to do is become friends with a few interracial couples and see how it works for them. It seems your mind has already been made up."

I didn't tell Chad there was someone else. I simply, and honestly, said I didn't feel I wanted to marry him. He was not visibly hurt at all. He even made a joke, "Do you think I could take that ring back to Jared?" We both laughed and hugged. I really did like him a lot.

And Michael...The first thing he did was come to my house and kisses me. A lot. Then he took me to dinner with his parents. His dad is a white man with a great wit. And my soon to be mother-in-law is a bit like my own Mother...rather stiff and pretentious.

We are definitely in love and it was the right decision. There is no boring, old married couple, routine lifestyle that I was so frightened of if I had married Chad. And the passion we have for everything we share makes even the ugliest day worth getting up for.

Mother has calmed down and although she is not going to invite any of her friends to the wedding, she sees my joy and is happy for me. Dad is my hero. He had my back when I needed him the most. I feel a different connection to him now than I had as a child. It is as if he shared a secret with me and our bond changed from father and child to confidants. Life is good....it's all good.

BETTE EPSTEIN

Author

Bette Epstein lives in Dallas, Texas with her big brown dog, Jake.

www.ingramcontent.com/pod-product-compliance
Lightning Source LLC
Chambersburg PA
CBHW071356310526
45789CB00020B/373